# SPIRIT BY THE SEA TRILOGY

## A NEW LIFE - BOOK ONE

## APRIL AUTRY

ALSO BY APRIL AUTRY

**Galactic Grandmother Past Life Series**

*ATLANTIS, JOURNEY FROM THE INNER TEMPLE*

*MY LIFE WITH JESUS*

*ESCAPE FROM MALDEK*

**Galactic Grandmother Spiritual Journey Series**

*WORKING IN THE QUANTUM FIELD, BOOK 1 & 2*

*MULTIDIMENSIONAL ASPECTS - HIGHER SELVES*

# CONTENTS

# CHAPTER 1

⁂

*I*n the blue sky, high above the clouds, I am weightless. I fly with ease through the vast infinite. My mind is calm and open to the wonder that surrounds me. I have no thoughts, just a feeling of total oneness with a universe bigger than my imagination. I do not see anyone, yet I know I am not alone. Then I hear a voice, "Look down."

I look down to see the earth, with swirls of white clouds over beautiful blue.

"I am taking you back," the voice said, and I begin to fly down.

I move quickly below the clouds and feel the earth reach out to me. Pulling me closer, I feel her warmth.

"She is alive!" I say and my heart warms from knowing this.

The blue of sea expands to the horizons on all sides. I see a green spot in the water, and as I come closer the ridges of jagged mountains appear. I am now above a high peak, watching water fall through the air into a pool far below.

The water draws me closer, and I look down to a figure sitting at the bottom beside the water. I see a small boy with black hair and skin darkened by the sun, and know it is me.

Suddenly I am back in my body. I take a gasp of air, wiggle my fingers and toes and feel the ground below me.

"We are with you." I hear the voice say.

I do not want to open my eyes. I hear a bird knocking on the tree behind me, the water falling hard into the pool, and the sun warms my face.

"A little longer," I think pinching my eyes closed.

"KAI!" I hear my brother call and open my eyes.

"Mother sends you to gather fruit and here you are!" Jatu kicks the empty basket on the ground and shakes his head. He stands looking at the water, then back at me.

"We will swim!" Jatu kicks off his sandals, and walks into the cool water of the pool, "then we pick fruit."

My legs are stiff as I stand up, and see the water sparkling, with light from the sun. Carefully stepping on the slippery rocks, I jump forward into the water joining my brother. Near the waterfall, we wrestle, pushing each other under the water. Laughing and gulping water as we do. My brother swims to the edge of the pool,

"We go," Jatu tells me as he steps from the water, "mother needs the fruit."

Jatu grabs the basket and walks down the path into the trees. I get out of the pool, stop to look at the water and up to the sky, then run into the trees behind him.

"I will live here." I tell him and put a fruit into the basket.

Jatu laughs, "You will live in the village, and fish with your brothers."

I shake my head and pick another fruit.

"The basket is full," Jatu said, and looks at me, "come."

He turns to walk down the muddy trail beside the stream. Trees block the sun over our heads as we walk through the ruins of our ancestors' village. Jatu stops at a stone wall, covered with green plants, and puts his hand on it.

"Thank you for this fruit."

I do the same, thinking of our ancestors that lived here, and how they ate fruit from the trees that now feed us. We reach our canoes pulled up out of the stream, and Jatu drops the basket of fruit down into his. Then he pushes his canoe into the water, jumps in and paddles with strength and quickness away from me. I push my canoe into the water, jump in, grab the paddle and move the canoe forward. The stream gets deeper, with tangled bushes and tree roots growing down on each side. I paddle toward the middle of the river, then the moving water catches the canoe and sends me toward the village. I stretch my legs out and look ahead. Jatu is already far down the river, I relax watching the birds fly in and out of trees.

"MY LITTLE TRAVELER," Mother said when she saw me, "come here."

She put her soft arms around me, squeezing me tight.

Jatu watched and shook his head, "He is not a baby!"

Mother let go and looked down at me, "Stay in the village."

I nodded.

"Help your father prepare for the feast."

I grabbed dried fish as I left our hut and walked to the sand. I saw my father, older brothers and many village men pulling in a large net full of fish from the water. There would be enough fish to feed all the villagers gathering this night for the ceremony. The net would need repair when they finished unloading it.

"I will do that."

BEING careful to weave the fishing net back into place, I held the net up, and checked for more holes.

"It is good," I thought.

I pulled two strips of palm leaf together, knotting it again, then wove the loose ends into the netting and stood up. The net was large and heavy. I looked across at another boy, weaving together holes from the many fish that were caught.

Our mothers were preparing the fish, and I would be glad to eat them. Some were hung up to dry, while others were kept in a basket under the water. I folded the net on itself, until it sat next to the boy.

"I will finish soon." he told me.

I stood up and looked around. "What next?"

I wanted to go back to the waterfall, yet I told my mother I would help. All the villagers were working, there would be no swimming or gathering shells this day. I looked forward to the feast, and the fire this night. A holy man from the other side of the island was coming. The village was happy, he would bless the village and ask the ancestors to join us. He also knew plant medicine, and guided the villagers.

The holy man had warned villagers to stop sleeping in the fishing huts along the river. He told us that after water fell from the sky, the river would grow big and carry much mud, trees, and rocks that would wash away the huts. They stopped sleeping there, and no villagers were hurt when the river tore down the fishing huts into the angry water.

The holy man healed sick villagers with plants, asked the ancestors to protect the village and guide them when they fished. For this, the fire would be big and there would be much celebration

I smelled fish on the fire, and my belly was hungry, so I walked back to mother.

"Your belly will not fill!" Mother said and laughed, "Here."

Mother had prepared fruits and fishes, that lay on palm leaves, and she handed me a fruit.

"Eat," she told me, "then gather wood for the fire pit."

I nodded as I bit into the sweet, juicy fruit. Mother turned to work, while I ate with juice running down my face and hands. I looked toward the sand, and saw men dragging large logs up to circle the fire pit. The circle was big, and every villager would join the feast. Only men and women sat on the logs, while children sat in the sand behind them.

The village fire pit was where the men spoke of fishing, and where we celebrated an elder's passing, a joining, or a new baby. The fire this night would be under a big moon and the holy man would speak. I wanted to see him and know more of him. Elders told us of seeing ancestors at the fire pit, after the holy man spoke.

I also had seen the ancestors around the fire pit and heard their voices. I heard a voice after swimming in the pool by the waterfall. I sat down in the sun to dry and closed my eyes. I felt peace, and the sound of the water made me want to sleep. Then I felt someone behind me, and quickly opened my eyes. Yet looking around, I saw no one. I closed my eyes again, then heard a voice.

"I will not hurt you."

I opened my eyes yet did not move. "Are you an ancestor?"

"Yes."

I was not afraid of the voice, it sounded like my grandfather that passed.

"I will speak with you again." the voice said.

After this, I left the village much to swim in the pool and sit by it. I closed my eyes and waited. Behind my closed eyes, I saw colors that swirled and changed shapes. I felt the sun and smelled the plants around me. The sound of the waterfall made me relax. Then a man's face came to me, he smiled and went away.

I wanted to see him again so I spent less time in the village, and more time going off by myself. I stopped fishing with my brothers, and stopped playing with the boys I had grown with. My father was not happy that I did this, yet mother told him,

"Let him go, he gathers fruit for me." I did not know then, that my mother also heard the ancestors speak.


THE FEAST WAS OVER. I had eaten so much fish and fruit that my belly hurt, and I stood rubbing it.

"You look like father!" Maka said, pointing to my belly, then ran away.

She stopped and looked back at me.

"My belly is too full to chase you!" I yelled.

My little sister liked me to chase her along the sand. We dug holes in it, and let the waves bring water into them. We gathered shells to make necklaces, swam in the waves and she wanted me to do this now. Maka made a face at me, then ran to find another to play with.

I stood near the circle of logs. Wood was piled high in the middle of the fire pit, yet would not be lit until the sun had gone behind the water. The big moon would be beautiful in the sky this night. I sat down on a log, faced the sea and looked out across to where the water met the sky. I wondered where the sky came from, and thought of flying through it. After seeing my island from above, I knew how small it is and how big the sea was. I wanted to learn much, yet I had not heard mother or father speak of this.

"Will the ancestor at the waterfall tell me?" I thought and I wondered if the holy man knew of these things.

I thought of the holy man when he arrived at the village. He was welcomed with flowers, fresh water and fruits. He was not an old man, he looked like my father yet did not have the lines around his eyes like father. He stood higher than most men, and he smiled when he saw us. His skin was dark from the sun, his hair was tied back, and he looked strong. He wore a cloth that hung from his waist, sandals and a clear stone that hung from woven string around his neck. He reached up much, to touch the stone when he spoke.

The holy man traveled with a younger man that was his assistant. They both carried baskets of medicines, water pouches and bed rolls. The holy man also carried a pouch, with things he used for the ceremonies, and he spread these out on a mat in the sun. The younger man watched over these, not letting the villagers touch them.

I waited for others to look, then I moved closer and squatted down to see them. There was a large dark feather, and a small pouch that was pulled together at the top. There was a half shell, with the colors of the sea that shined inside. There were dried plant leaves rolled up, and bound with string, I bent down, breathed in and they smelled good. A pile of necklaces made from sea shells and seeds lay next to the dried plants. I saw the holy man give these to villagers, I did not know why he gave these away, yet I wanted to get a necklace from him. I looked up and saw the assistant watching me.

"Where do you live?" I asked.

"On the other side"

"Is your village big?"

"We do not live in a village."

"Where do you live?"

"A camp on the side of a mountain," he told me, "it was built by the ancestors for their holy man."

"Oh," I had not known this.

"All holy men and their assistants have lived there."

"Why do you live with him?" I asked.

"He teaches me to make medicines."

I pulled my eyebrows together and thought of this.

"He shows me the plants to gather, and how to prepare them. He knows which medicines to give the villagers, and how to bring in the ancestors for healing."

I nodded, "This is good."

The assistant smiled at me.

"Does he teach you to speak to the ancestors?" I asked.

He nodded his head.

"How long have you lived with the holy man?"

"Since I was a boy."

"Is he the only holy man on the island?"

I felt a large, warm hand on my shoulder. I turned to see the holy man looking down on me.

"What is your name?" he asked.

"Ka, Kai." I said, and felt my face get warm.

"Kai," he said and smiled, "I am the only medicine man on this island."

"There are medicine women." I said, thinking of the women that help bring in babies, "they give medicine to the new mothers."

"Yes," he told me, "a medicine woman also helps me."

"Where is she?" I asked, "I did not see her."

"She comes when I need her."

I remembered the voice that spoke to me. "She is an ancestor?"

"You have heard the ancestors?" The holy man said.

"Yes."

He bent down close to me and I looked into his dark eyes, then he nodded.

"I will speak with you again," he said and stood up. He reached his hand down to pull me up.

"Go enjoy yourself." He told me.

I wanted to stay, yet I knew he was asking me to leave. I walked away, stopped to look back and saw the assistant looking at me as the holy man spoke.


"WE GO." the holy man told the villagers.

He walked on the path by the river, followed by elder men and my father. Mother walked with the older women, then younger men, women and children followed behind. The holy man stopped and looked at the water. He raised his arms up to the sky and closed his eyes. The villagers walked to stand behind him.

"Great Father we thank you for this day. We thank you for the sun that warms us, and the moon that gives us light in the night."

He took in a long deep breath.

"Great Mother we thank you for the water in the river and sea. We thank you for the fruit and fish that you feed us."

The holy man opened his eyes and squatted down beside to the river. He opened the pouch that was tied at the top, grabbed dried flowers from it and threw them on the water. I heard him speaking softly to the river yet did not know what he said. He washed his hands in the water, stood and signaled for a grandfather to come to him. The holy man put his hands on the old man's shoulders, closed his eyes and stood quietly. Then he opened his eyes and smiled at the grandfather,

"Enjoy your blessings."

The old man nodded and put his hand up to rest on the holy man's arm,

"Thank you."

The holy man dropped his hands and the grandfather looked back at us with a smile, then walked down the trail toward the fire pit. Now each villager waited to step forward for the holy man to bless. He put his hands on each one, closing his eyes and standing quietly before he spoke to them.

Finally, I stood in front of the holy man. He laid his hands on my shoulders and closed his eyes. I felt heat coming from his hands as they rested on me. Then he raised his hands, and looked into my eyes, "Live well."

I had not heard such a beautiful voice, it seemed to carry music with it.

"Was this the man that spoke to me before?" I thought and did not move.

I felt a small push from behind and turned to see a boy waiting. He stepped beside me, to stand in front of the holy man. I moved back, watched the holy man put his hands on the boy's shoulders, then I walked down the trail.

I looked ahead and saw bright colors of ripe fruit over the sea. The sun was low to the water, I felt happy and full of peace.

"Thank you!" I thought, knowing the holy man would also be thankful for the beautiful sky. He made me think of this in a new way. Then I thought of the fire pit and began to run down the path. I wanted to sit close behind the logs, so I could hear what the holy man said to the ancestors.

Flames rose high, and the villagers gathered around the fire pit to watch the holy man. When he joined us, he was happy and laughed much. Then he raised his arms and asked the ancestors to come.

"Join us this night." he said loudly.

I looked around at the villagers sitting on logs, or standing.

"Protect the village and guide the men when they fish."

"Yes!" a man called out.

I looked to him and in the darkness behind, I saw ancestors.

The holy man looked around, "They are here," he nodded, "speak to those that have passed."

While villagers began to speak to their ancestors, the holy man stepped to a man and walked with him down by the water. When they returned, the holy man took an old woman, to stand away from the others to speak with. Then the holy man walked back with the old woman and pointed toward me. I sat in the sand behind my mother, and I turned my head to see where he pointed. The villagers also turned to look where the holy man pointed. The holy man walked to me and put out his hand. My mouth fell open as I reached up to him. He pulled me up, and we walked to the wet sand by the water.

I looked at him, saw him watching the light from the big moon fall on the water, then he looked at me.

"Are you happy?" he asked.

I did not know what to say and was quiet.

"Do you want to fish, and live in the village with your family?"

I shook my head, "I do not like to fish."

"What do you enjoy?"

"I like to sit by the waterfall."

"The ancestors speak to you there?"

I looked up at him and nodded.

"Do you play in the ancestors' village?" he asked.

My eyes grew wide and wondered how he knew this.

"When I was young," he told me, "I played with a boy who was an ancestor."

"You did?'

"Yes."

"I hear them." I told him.

He looked at me and put his hand on my shoulder. "Have you traveled away from your village?"

"No."

He squatted down, looking into my eyes, "Do you want to leave your village?"

My eyes opened wide and I looked back at him.

"You would leave your family to learn from me."

"Like your assistant?"

"Yes, you would learn from Konani also."

"Konani?"

"That is his name."

I never thought of leaving my village or leaving mother, yet I wanted to go.

"Yes" I said, "I will go."

He did not smile. "You will not see your mother," he said, "think on this."

"I will go," I told him, "I want to learn."

The holy man looked at me yet did not speak. I waited, looking at his face, then he stood up.

"I will speak to your father." The holy man said and turned to walk back.

I stood there and he waved to me, "Come."

I followed him back to the fire pit, and saw mother looking at me with water in her eyes. She patted the log by her, and she put out her arms and pulled me to her. She squeezed me tight and when I started to pull away, she would not let me go. She held my hand and made me sit by her.


WHEN THE SUN ROSE, the holy man sat with my father and mother. He told them the ancestors had guided him to our village to find his new assistant.

"When I saw Kai talking to my assistant, I knew he was the boy I would teach."

My father looked at me, "He does not like to fish," then he put his hand on my arm, "Do you want to learn medicine?"

I looked at mother, then back at him and nodded.

"Where will you take him?" my father asked.

"To the mountain camp on the other side of the island. I live there with my assistant."

"Will we see him?"

"He can return when he wants," the holy man said, and looked at me, "yet learning medicine will take many big moons."

Mother looked at me with water in her eyes, "My grandmother, who lives with the ancestors, told me of this."

The holy man looked at her and nodded, "Kai is guided by the ancestors."

Father slapped his leg with his hand, "Kai will be a medicine man!" he smiled at me, and looked at the holy man, "We are blessed that you will teach him."

The holy man smiled back at my father, "I am blessed."


THE HOLY MAN, and Konani, ate with my family. Mother packed dried fish and fruit for me, father gave me a bed roll and a water pouch. Many villagers stood outside my hut, waiting to see the holy man. Father hung the bed roll over my shoulder, and mother put the food in a pouch that hung from it. Maka walked to me, and put her arms out. I put my arms around her, looked over to see Jatu, and my older brothers watching.

"I will return." I said, and rubbed my sister's hair.

My mother grabbed me, and spoke softly in my ear, "Be safe."

Then my father clapped me on the arm, "Travel well." he said loudly, so the villagers also heard him.

I walked out of the hut behind the holy man, and his assistant. The sun was rising from behind the mountain, and I waved at my family, then the surprised villagers as we walked away.


NOW THE SUN was over my head, and we had not stopped walking, since we left my village. The holy man walked ahead on the trail, followed by Konani, and I walked slowly behind him. I had not walked so far up the side of a mountain, and my legs hurt with every step. I walked on a muddy trail, looking down to place my feet safely, not wanting to step off the trail and fall down the mountain.

"We stop soon." Konani called back.

"I am tired!" I thought, and felt the bed roll pull hard on my shoulder.

I shook my head, and wanted to stop, yet kept walking. I moved my bed roll to the other shoulder, and felt the pouch with food against my arm. My belly was hungry.

"I want to eat," I thought, and saw myself return to my village, where mother would feed me.

"Watch your step." Konani yelled.

I stopped and looked at the narrow trail ahead, it hung on the side of the steep mountain. Water trickled down over the trail, I knew it would be hard to walk over and not slip. I did not want to jump across it, so I slowly put one foot down, and pushed into the mud until I felt safe to stand. Then did the same with the next foot, again and again until I reached the other side. Konani stood watching me, then turned to walk away. I looked down the side of the mountain, and wondered where the holy man's camp was. I thought of mother, the waterfall I enjoyed, and wondered why I left. Konani was now far ahead, I felt the mud on my feet and sandals.

"I will go back." I thought.

"The ancestors guide you."

I knew that voice, "You are with me?"

"We are with you."

I took in a big breath, and blew it out. The ancestors had told the holy man he would teach me, and grandmother had told mother.

"The ancestors are guiding me," I thought.

I turned my head to look out across the sea, to where it joined with the sky. I thought of flying over it, and knew I was not to live in my small village. I looked back at the trail, and took a step.

"I begin my new life."

# CHAPTER 2

We had traveled far from my village, and when I looked back, I could not see it. The trail followed the mountain, turning many times away from the sea, then back again. We are high up, and I think of when I saw these mountains from the sky. Ahead the trail is going down, where it widens, then goes into trees.

"We rest under the trees." the holy man called back.

"Good." I walk faster, to be close behind Konani.

"Sit," the holy man says, "we eat."

I slide the bedroll off my shoulder, let it drop to the ground, and it feels good to have the weight off. Then I dropped down, sat on my bedroll, and reached quickly for the food my mother packed. Pulling out a piece of dry fish, I put it to my mouth,

"Wait Kai!" Konani said, "Do not eat."

I took the fish from my lips, and feel water in my mouth. The holy man and Konani sit down on their bed rolls.

The holy man looked at me, "Kai, look around. Look at the sky, with no water clouds. Look at the trees, that give us shade, and fruit to eat."

I saw many fruit on the trees, and nodded my head.

"Look at the fish in your hand." he said, "Your mother prepared that for you."

I swallowed, felt water in my eyes, and wondered when I would see her again.

"We thank the Great Father and Mother for our blessings."

Konani closed his eyes.

"We thank you for this good day to travel, we thank you for giving us shade to rest, and we thank you for the food we eat." he said.

I watched the holy man take a bite of fruit, and quickly bit into my fish. It tasted of the sea, and made me think of mother. I had watched her cut the fish into strips many times, then hang them up to dry. Now I sat here, far from her, eating them. When we finished, Konani waved for me to come with him.

"We get water"

I stood up to follow.

"Here." the holy man gave me his pouch to fill, then I walked off behind Konani.


I LIKED WALKING under the trees, listening to the birds sing, and watching them fly. We stopped at a rock wall, and I looked up where the mountain met the sky. Konani walked to a small stream, that poured from a crack in the rocks. I waited for Konani to get a drink and fill his water pouch, then I put my free hand under the water, and scooped it into my mouth. It was cold and tasted good, I put the holy man's pouch under the water and filled it, then mine. I laid the pouches down, and used both hands to scoop up water to wash my face.

"Good, huh?" Konani said.

I looked at him with a wet face, and smiled.

"How are you?" Konani asked.

"Good."

"We will walk much, before we stop to sleep." he told me.

"I am ready." After having my bedroll off my shoulder, and filling my belly, I was ready to see where the trail would take us.

. . .

WE TRAVELED FAR, and now sat around a small fire. My body was tired, it felt good to sit on my bed roll, and watch the flames. My eyes were heavy, and I thought of Mother. After she fed us, I would lay on my mat next to Jatu, and she sang to us as we fell asleep. I awoke when the sun rose, mother fed us again, and I felt safe when she wrapped her soft arms around me. Water came into my eyes, I wanted to see Mother.

"You will feel good after you sleep." the holy man said.

I looked from the fire, to the holy man, who was watching me.

"It is hard to leave your family." He told me .

I nodded my head.

"We will sleep."

I watched the holy man, and Konani, lay their bed rolls back from the fire, and I did the same. I watched Konani kick dirt on the fire, then turned on my side, and closed my eyes.


"WAKE!" Konani shook my shoulder. I was dreaming of playing in the waves with my sister.

"Where am I?" I thought, and rubbed my eyes.

"Get up! We eat and leave"

I sat up, scratched my head, and yawned. The fire was blazing again, and a small pot sat close to the flames. I got to my knees, rolled up the bedroll, then tied it with a reed rope. I reached for my pouch, and looked at the dried fruit and fish inside.

"I have fruit and tea for you." Konani told me.

I nodded, and looked around for the holy man.

Konani saw me. "He watches the sun come up."

Konani pulled dried fruit, and nuts from a pouch. It looked good, and my stomach made noise.

"Do you have a shell?"

"Yes." I reached inside my food pouch, where mother had put a half shell big enough to drink from. I handed it to Konani.

"We wait." he said, sat down on his bed roll, and looked up. I looked up also, then back at Konani, whose eyes were closed. I watched him breath in slowly, then breath out slowly. Konani sat quietly, not moving.

"Oh," I thought, "I do that by the waterfall."

I closed my eyes, breathed in and out, and felt relaxed. Inside my head, I saw trees beside a mountain. I walked by a river, to a clearing where huts circled a small fire pit. I heard steps, and opened my eyes, to see the holy man standing on the other side of the fire. He was smiling and his eyes were bright.

"Are you hungry?" Konani asked.

"Yes." he said, and sat down on his bedroll.

Konani grabbed pieces of palm leaves, and put fruit and nuts on them. He handed them to the holy man, and me. Then he used another palm leaf, folded over, to lift the pot from the fire pit. Konani carefully poured tea into the half shells, and gave them to us.

"Thank you." the holy man said, as Konani sat down.

"Thank you ancestors for this food." The holy man said, picked up fruit, and put it in his mouth.

"Good!" he told Konani.

I was glad to eat, and put a handful of fruit and nuts into my mouth. After finishing the fruit and nuts, I picked up my shell with both hands. The shell was hot from the tea water, I put my lips to it, and sipped. The tea washed the sweetness of the fruit from my mouth. My belly was not full, so I grabbed dried fish and fruit from my pouch.

"You eat much!" Konani said.

"You will be happy this night." the holy man told me.

I looked at him, then he and Konani laughed.

Konani nodded, "This night you will be happy."


WE WALKED along the top of the mountains. There were no trees this high, and no shade to keep us cool. The sun was hot on my face and shoulders, and the holy man stopped so we could drink from our pouches, then we walked on. The bedroll dug into the top of my shoulder, and my legs hurt with each step. We stopped to eat, and I was glad to sit, yet the rest was short. Soon we walked on the trail, with the holy man far ahead, and Konani in front of me. I stopped, and drank from my water pouch. Konani stopped, and turned around.

"Do not stop," he said, "keep walking."

I nodded, he looked at me, "Keep walking." he said again, and turned to walk ahead.

I walked slower, and slower. My legs got harder and harder to pick up, and put down. The holy man was gone from my sight, and now I did not see Konani. Water ran down my face, and I wanted to stop, yet I kept walking. I did not know how long I could do this.

"When will we get to the camp?" I wiped water from my face, and looked ahead. The trail turned behind the mountain, and as I walked around it, I saw the holy man and Konani waiting for me.


"TAKE HIS BED ROLL." the holy man told Konani.

Konani took the bedroll from my shoulder, and my shoulder raised up from the weight taken off.

"Drink." the holy man said, and I took a drink from my water pouch.

"I am slow." I told him.

He laughed, "We are all slow when we are young! You are not strong yet."

We started to walk again, and I watched Konani carry my bedroll.

"Thank you." I told him, and was glad it was not pulling down on my shoulder.

The trail slowly wound down the mountain, and I smelled the sea on the wind. My legs hurt, yet as I watched the sun go down, I knew we would leave the mountain soon. We reached flat land, and the trail led us under trees toward the water.

. . .

THE HOLY MAN spoke to Konani quietly, and I could not hear what he said. Then I heard children laughing. My eyes searched the trail ahead, yet I saw only trees. I heard men talking now.

"A village!" I cried out.

I followed them into the clearing outside a village. Children laughed as they ran beside us, their mothers smiled and waved, as we passed huts where they worked. We were welcomed, and the villagers were happy to see the holy man. He greeted the men by placing his hand on their shoulder, and saying their name. We were led to sand shaded by palm trees, given water and fruit, then told of the fish we would eat later at a feast.

I sat down and rested my legs. I watched children playing in the waves, digging in the sand, and I thought of my village. I saw men bringing firewood to the fire pit, which was already circled with logs for sitting. We leaned against the palm trees, enjoying the rest, and I was happy that we would be eating a feast this night.

The color of the sky changed, mixing with the clouds over the water, as the sun fell into the sea. It was beautiful to watch, yet my eyes felt heavy, and I let them close. I awakened with Konani shaking my shoulder, it was getting dark.

"The holy man blesses the food."

I stood up, and Konani looked at me, "Eat all they give you."

I nodded, and followed him, to stand behind the villagers at the fire pit.

We listened to the holy man speak a blessing for the villagers, the food, and fishing. Konani grabbed my arm, we walked through the villagers to stand by the holy man, then we sat down. Women were taking fish from the fire pit, and they smelled good. Soon the women brought palm leaves piled with hot fish, and other palm leaves piled with cold fish, and fruit. I watched the holy man take some of all the fish and fruit, then passed it to Konani, who did the same, and passed it to me. I took fish and fruit, placing it on a palm leaf sitting on my legs, and looked up. The villagers watched and smiled, as I passed it to the man sitting next to me. When I ate all the fish and fruit, my belly was full, and the villagers were glad I liked it.

"He eats much!" a villager said.

I looked at Konani, he nodded, and smiled at me.

AFTER EATING, the holy man spoke with the men, and Konani left to ask villagers if they needed medicine. I sat by the fire, and thought of my village. I wondered when I would see my family again, I thought of the medicine camp we traveled to, and wondered how long I would be there. The villagers here looked happy.

"Was I happy in my village?" I wondered, "why did I want to leave the village to play, or sit by the waterfall?"

I thought on this, "I did not want to fish with my father and brothers, I did not want to play warrior, and fight with the boys."

"It is good you left." A voice in my head said.

"Yes." I thought, "yet the traveling is hard."

NIGHT CAME OVER US, and the women and children had gone to their huts. The holy man still spoke with men at the fire pit, Konani had not returned, so I walked toward the water to look at the sea, when suddenly I tripped over some legs.

"Ouch!" a small voice called out.

I fell on the sand, then sat up, brushing sand from my arms and chest.

"I did not see you!" I said.

"Watch where you walk!" the small voice yelled, and I saw her sit up in the darkness.

She was small, and I asked, "Why are you here?"

"When it is night, I watch the lights in the sky."

"Oh" I said. "I will watch with you."

She did not answer, and lay back down on the warm sand. I lay down next to her, and looked up. I also did this in my village.

"What is your name?"

"Kai, what is yours?"

"Milana."

"Malana?"

"No, Milana," she said again.

I watched the lights in the sky, and enjoyed the sound of the waves.

"Are you going to live with the holy man?"

"Yes."

"I want to live with the holy man," she said, "yet grandfather said I cannot leave!"

"Oh" I wondered why a young girl wanted to leave her village.

"I saw the holy man when he came down from his camp, you were not with him."

"He came to our village for a feast, and said he would teach me medicine."

Milana sat up, "He asked you?"

"Yes."

She waved her arms in the air, "Why did the holy man ask you?"

She leaned down close to my face, and looked at me. I saw her bright eyes shining. "I want to learn medicine!" she said, and fell back on to the sand, "I want to speak to the ancestors!"

"I hear the ancestors." I told her.

She sat up, and looked at me again, "Do you speak to them?"

"No."

"Oh!" she said, and lay back down.

"I want to train with the holy man," Milana said, "I want to learn all he does!"

I listened to her, and thought, "She does not know leaving your family is hard."

Milana suddenly jumped up, "He asked you! You will not be a good medicine man, if you cannot speak to the ancestors!"

"I will learn!" I told her.

I looked up at this little girl standing next to me. She put her hands on her hips,

"I would be a good assistant!"

"You are still a girl." I spoke softly, thinking she was too young to train.

"Oh!" Milana screamed, "He will train me, and I will be a medicine woman!" Then she turned quickly, and ran down the beach toward some huts. I sat up, and watched her run away.

"I have not met a girl such as this," and shook my head.

I lay back down on the sand, with my hands behind my head, and looked up at the stars. After watching the night sky, I returned to my bed roll, and slept hard without dreams.


THE SUN, and sounds from the village, woke me. I rubbed my eyes, and sat up. Two bedrolls were beside mine, neatly tied, yet I had not known the holy man or Konani slept next to me during the night.

"I was tired" I thought, and looked for them among the villagers. I saw Konani sitting on a log by the campfire, eating.

"Fish!" I jumped out of my bed roll, leaving it spread out, and ran to Konani.

"Hungry?" Konani asked.

I nodded my head, and Konani handed me the bag with fruit and nuts.

"Eat quickly, we leave soon."

I put a handful of dried fruit and nuts into my mouth, and began chewing. I looked around for the small girl I met the night before.

"Milana" I said to myself, saying it the way she taught me.

I looked at the huts, did not see her, then turned to watch Konani. My mouth was full, as I chewed. He filled his shell with tea from a pot on the fire, and handed it to me.

"Thank you" I said, and sipped it.

"After you eat, wash over there," he pointed to a stream of water coming down to the sea, "get ready to leave."

I did as he said, then went back to my bed roll. I was rolling it up, and saw Milana down by the water. I waved to her, she did not smile, and ran away.

I shook my head, "I do not know why she does this!"

· · ·

THE VILLAGERS WAITED to see us leave, an elder asked the holy man to return at the next big moon, for a feast in the village.

"I will not return," the holy man told him, "yet I will ask the ancestors to be with you."

The elder nodded, and was happy with this. The holy man smiled, and waved to the villagers, then we walked out of the village. I carried my own bed roll, and it did not feel heavy. The feast and sleep had prepared me for a day of travel. I felt good as I walked behind the holy man and Konani. The sky was clear, and a warm wind blew from the water. I had enjoyed seeing a new village, and was ready to see more of the island.

"This is a good day to travel," the holy man said, "we are blessed."

I smiled, and enjoyed the walk. The sun rose over us, as we followed the trail just above the sea. I watched the waves crash below us, saw big birds dive in to catch fish, then sit on the rolling water to eat. The trail took us slowly up, the air became cooler, and clouds hung over the top of the mountain. The smell of flowers was in the air, and I looked ahead, wanting to see where we went. Konani told me we would reach the medicine man's camp before dark.

WE STOPPED TO EAT, yet did not rest. We walked up and across the side of the mountain, then turned, and walked up and across the other way. My legs started to hurt again, and the bedroll was pulling down on my shoulder. I felt pain go down my back, yet I would not ask for help.

"I do not want Konani to carry my bedroll!" I said quietly, and pushed my legs to move under me.

"We are close to the top!" Konani called back.

I took in a big breath, looked ahead, and still saw a lot of trail to walk. "I will keep going," I thought, "I can do this."

. . .

AT THE TOP, I joined the holy man and Konani, to look at a valley below. The valley stretched out to meet the sand, and water with small waves. I did not see a village.

"There is no village?"

"Ancestors lived there," the holy man said, "when a wave came that washed the village away."

"Oh." I wondered how big the wave was.

"It is a burial site now," the holy man told me.

Konani pointed to a waterfall at the back of the valley, "the camp is there."

"The ancestors built a hut for their holy man," the holy man said, "all holy men have lived there, and taught assistants there."


I FOLLOWED them down into the valley, as we went the sun dropped lower. Back under the trees now, the light was leaving, and we walked faster. The trail led us to the waterfall, and I heard water pounding on the rocks as we got closer. Then I saw it. I stretched my neck to look up, the water fell from high on the mountain, down into a pool surrounded by rocks.

"We go up!" Konani told me.

I watched the holy man and Konani climb up beside the waterfall, carefully grabbing large rocks to pull up, and climbing between them toward the top. I followed, and stretched my arms and legs high, yet could not climb as they did. Konani turned, gave me his hand many times, lifting me up to stand by him. I watched the holy man, he climbed on steps cut into the mountain. He held branches from nearby trees and bushes, as he climbed up the narrow stone and dirt steps. Konani and I followed, and my legs screamed with each step. I looked down at my leg, and watched it twitch, as I leaned forward on it. I had to stop, then looked down. We were almost to the top of the waterfall, and I knew a bad step would send me falling down. I held tight to a tree branch while pulling myself up to the next step, then grabbed another branch, and pulled myself up again. I looked up, and saw Konani, reaching down to me. I stretched my arm up to him, he grabbed my hand, and lifted me to the top.

"Is there no other way?" I asked.

"There is a trail, on the other side of the camp, it is also hard."

"The holy men were well protected" I said.

"Yes!" Konani said, and laughed.

I looked around, and saw that we stood on a flat area, next to a river. The river ran smoothly, then fell down the waterfall. Large rocks lay in the water, making deep pools, with light shining on them. Many plants, and bushes with flowers, grew by the river. I breathed in deep, and smelled sweetness in the air. This place held good feelings, and peace. I looked away from the river, and saw huts under the trees.

"Is this the camp?" I asked, feeling happy.

Konani nodded, "Yes."

# CHAPTER 3

*I* awoke to someone wiggling my toe. I opened my eyes, looked up, and saw the thatched roof of the hut I shared with Konani. I sat up, looked down to my feet, no one stood there. Through the dim light of early morning, I saw Konani sleeping, on his mat across the room. I looked hard at him, to see if he was playing, yet Konani was asleep.

"I am tired!" I thought.

I lay back down, and closed my eyes. I was tired from the long walk, and I was in a hut far from my mother. She would not give me food, or wrap her arms around me, and she would not care for me. I would have to care for myself now, and I felt far away from her.

"YOU WILL REST THIS DAY," the holy man said as he ate his food, "Konani will show you the camp."

We ate fresh fruit, berries and nuts. I ate until I was full, then was given tea. Konani and I sat on a log, in the center of the clearing. In front of us was a fire pit, ringed with rocks, and a cooking pole stretched across the fire. There were huts under the trees around us. The large hut belonged to the holy man, and I was told not to enter it. The hut I shared with Konani was across the clearing from the holy man, there was a hut for travelers, and a small hut for storing food.

"Do not bring food into our sleeping hut," Konani said, "we eat at the fire pit, then clean."

After we finished eating, he waved me to follow him. He washed the tea pot in the river, filled it with fresh water, then put it back in the fire pit. We took the palm leaves that held our food, and threw them in the fire. Then Konani grabbed the basket with berries and nuts, and led me to the small hut.

"The food is kept here." he told me.

He opened the door, and I saw dried fruit, baskets of green leaves, plants, flowers and fish, all hanging from the top of the hut. The small hut was full.

"The holy man keeps food for travel here, and for when water clouds come."

I looked up.

"Clouds with much water come to the camp," Konani said, and stepped back to close the door.

"We will swim"

I nodded, and followed Konani to the pools of water, then we climbed out on a large rock.

"It is deep here."

I looked at the pool of water, where it was held by the rocks, then further across to the strong water that ran over the falls.

"Stay out of the river" Konani said, "the holy man said to swim in these pools, on this side of the river."

"I will."

Konani said this again, "You will not swim away from these pools."

"Yes," I said, and nodded.

Then Konani jumped into the water, he went under, and he came up smiling.

"I like to swim here." he told me.

I climbed to the same rock, and jumped. I went under the water, my feet did not touch the bottom, then came up for air.

I laughed and Konani jumped from the rock next to me, splashing water in my face.

We swam, laughed, and I enjoyed this much. When we finished swimming, we lay on the rocks to dry in the sun. The dirt was washed from me, and I felt good.

"I will show you where to gather food and fish," Konani said.

"What does the holy man do here?" I asked.

"The holy man leaves camp to watch the sun rise, and speak to the ancestors. He comes back to eat, then he takes us to learn which plants to pick for medicine."

Konani turned over on the rock, and looked at me.

"After we gather plants, he prepares medicines, weaves baskets and makes necklaces. He will teach you all he does."

I turned on my belly, and looked at him.

"When the sun has gone down, we start a fire, and eat. After we have cleaned, we sit by the fire pit, and wait for the ancestors to join us." Konani told me.

I nodded.

"The ancestors told the holy man to bring you here."

I sat up, and looked at him, "they told him to bring me?"

"They told him to get me also."

"Did he teach other assistants?" I asked.

"He did," Konani said, "then he sent them to another island."

"Another island?" I cried out, "Where?"

"Across the water from the village where we slept last night."

I had not seen an island across the sea, not even from up on the mountain.

"It is far away." I said.

"Yes, the assistants had to build a long boat to get there."

I shook my head, I did not know I would be sent away, and I do not want to go to a new island!

"Why did he send them away?"

"He taught them all he knows, and the ancestors guide them now."

"I wonder if they got to the island safely." I shook my head, thinking of going in a boat, across the sea.

"He said they are happy. One has joined, and has children, the other chooses not to join."

"Did they come back?" I asked.

"No, the ancestors show the holy man in his dreams."

My belly felt sick thinking of this. The ancestors told the holy man to take me from my village, and after I am trained, the holy man will send me away. I was not happy!

"Will he send you away?" I asked.

Konani laughed, "I will not leave soon, I have much to learn."

"Good." I said.


I FOLLOWED Konani around this day, yet my head was full of thoughts. I had been glad to learn from the holy man, now I wondered when I would be sent away, and where. Father told me of warriors on other islands, and I did not want to go there.

"Should I go back?" I thought, yet to travel to my village, would be long and hard. My father would not be happy to see me return, he was honored by his son learning to be a medicine man.

"Mother would be happy." I thought, yet I knew I would not go. My heart was heavy, thinking of what I had done. Leaving with the holy man had felt good, now it did not.

As darkness fell on us, we watched the fire.

"I gathered a large basket of new medicine leaves," the holy man told us, "and hung them in the food hut to dry."

"When the sun rises, I will take you to gather," he said, "then show you which plants to mix for medicine."

I watched the hot wood in the fire, listening to him speak.

"I have much to learn," I thought, "I will not leave soon."


KONANI HAD TAKEN me to fish in the river this day, and now the holy man cooked them on sticks over the fire. These fish were smaller than sea fish, and when the skin was brown, he slid them off on to a palm leaf. He covered the fish with a pile of green leaves, then the leaves turn soft from the hot fish. I waited for the holy man to say a blessing.

The holy man looked at Konani and me, "I am happy to be back in the old camp."

He smiled, took in a big breath, and closed his eyes.

"Thank you Father and Mother for bringing us here again. Thank you for our safe travel, and for this fish that will fill our bellies. Help Kai learn much, and be happy."

He opened his eyes, smiled, and looked at me. "Are you ready to eat?"

I nodded, and Konani laughed, "He is always ready to eat!"

Konani and the holy man laughed. My mouth filled with water looking at the fish, yet I waited for the holy man to take a bite. He leaned forward and grabbed some fish and leaves between his fingers, and put it in his mouth.

"Good!" he said, and Konani took a bite also. I grabbed the fish and leaves between my fingers, and put it in my mouth.

I nodded my head, "Good!"

The holy man and Konani laughed again. We ate until there was no more fish and leaves, then Konani gave us sweet, juicy berries, and tea. I enjoyed this food much, and my belly was full. Konani and I cleaned, then sat down by the fire pit.

The holy man took in a long deep breath, and slowly blew it out from his mouth. I looked over to see the him sitting with his eyes closed, then as he started another slow deep breath, Konani joined him. They breathed in together, held the breath in their bodies, then slowly pushed all the air out. Again, they breathed in, then out. I breathed in, and breathed out with them. The holy man opened his eyes, and looked across the fire toward the darkness.

"Thank you for being with us. Thank you for guiding us, and protecting us."

I looked across the fire pit, into the darkness, and saw men with tall head dresses of feathers.

"These ancestors are not as the ancestors in my village." I thought.

I looked at the holy man, and his eyes were closed again. I looked back to the ancestors, and heard a voice in my head.

"We help you."

I sat quietly, and watched the ancestors go back into the darkness. I waited for the holy man, and Konani, to open their eyes.

Finally, the holy man opened his eyes, and smiled at me.

"They are glad you are here"

"Me?"

"Yes," he said, "they waited for you to come."

"I saw them."

"I will teach you to hear them also" the holy man said.

"I heard them," I told him, "they said we help you."

The holy man nodded. "This is good. You learn fast."

"I do not want to learn fast!" I thought, "I do not want to go to another island!"

The holy man pulled his eyebrows together, and turned to Konani.

"They told me a man travels here, and that we will travel also."

"I will prepare." Konani said, then looked at me, "I will wake you to fish."

I nodded my head.

"I sleep now." The holy man said, and stood up.

I watched him walk into his hut.

"We will sleep also." Konani said.

I lay down on my mat, and put my hands behind my head. Konani was on his mat, turned on his side, to face me.

"Did you see the ancestors?" I asked Konani

"Yes."

"Do you hear them?"

"Yes."

"What do they say?"

"They say, sleep well." Konani smiled, and closed his eyes.

"I like the medicine man's camp." I thought, "We swam and fished, ate good food, and saw the ancestors by the fire pit."

I closed my eyes to sleep, saw mother's face smiling at me, then she went away.

"Mother." I whispered, "you are with me."

My heart felt warm, and peace came over me. In my head, I saw my village, and soon fell asleep.

WE WALKED UNDER TREES, the branches spread out over our heads, covering us from the sun. The holy man had filled his basket with many plants.

"Gather these." he said, and showed me a leaf.

"There!" Konani pointed to a bush, nodding his head for me to pick there. Then he walked down the trail, and the holy man went back to camp.

I picked the leaves, and looked around. I enjoyed this, and wanted to learn how to prepare medicine with these leaves.

"I want your help." I told the ancestors, "I ask you to guide me, so I will learn much."

I felt the sun, looked up to see it shining through the trees, and the leaves seemed to whisper, "We will guide you."

"Kai!" Konani called.

I stood still, listening to where Konani's call came from.

"Kai!" Konani yelled.

I ran toward him, wondering if he was hurt.

I found him smiling, and pointing down. "Look what I found!"

I looked down at the dirt by the roots of a tree, and saw small round plants growing.

"They are used by the mountain village for a spirit ceremony." Konani said, and squatted down.

"I will pick these, and wash my hands."

"Do they make you sick?" I asked.

"Yes, the holy man will prepare these for the spirit ceremony."

I squatted down, and looked at them.

I watched, as he cut the plants with a blade, and put them beside the leaves in his basket.

I showed him my basket.

"Good," he said, "we will return, and show the holy man what I found!"


As we walked through the trees, Konani pointed to plants we would gather later.

"The holy man will teach you how to prepare them."

When the trail neared the camp, we heard laughter.

"It's Kekoa!" Konani said, and walked fast down the trail.

"Kekoa?"

"He is a great warrior from another island."

"Why is he here?" I asked, thinking of the warriors my father spoke of.

Konani called over his shoulder "He came here after a battle on his island, and the holy man healed his wounds."

"Will he leave?"

"No, he has a family in a village now."


I followed Konani, and thought of this. "A village I have not seen."

"Where is this village?" I thought, "what other villages will I see?"

Closer to the camp, Konani began to run and laugh, "Kekoa!" he cried out.

"Konani!" said a big voice.

I walked into the camp, and saw a large man standing with his arms around Konani, lifting him off the ground. The man set him down, held Konani back and looked up, then down.

"You grow big!" he said.

Konani looked up at Kekoa, "No man is big like you!"

Kekoa slapped Konani's arm hard, and laughed loud.

I walked next to the holy man, and stopped. Kekoa turned his head, looked at me, and smiled.

"A new boy?"

The holy man pushed me forward, "My new assistant, Kai."

Kekoa walked to me, I had not seen a man this big, and my mouth fell open. His chest was wide, with black marks drawn on his skin. His shoulders had the black marks, also his strong arms that swung as he walked. I saw a long line across his belly, where a wound had healed. His hair was pulled back into a tie, and he wore a cloth that hung from his waist. As he walked to me, his big feet hit the ground hard, and he stopped in front of me, looking down.

"You will learn medicine?" he asked.

"Yes." I said, looking up at him.

"Learn well from the holy man, " he said, "he healed me."

I looked again at the wound mark on his belly.

"I will also teach you." he told me.

I looked up to his face, his dark eyes watched me.

"You will teach me medicine?"

Kekoa leaned his head back, and laughed loud, "No!"

I looked at the holy man.

"He will teach you many things." the holy man said.

Konani spoke to me, "He will teach you to fight as a warrior!"

"Oh." I looked back at Kekoa, who stood with his hands on his hips.

The holy man nodded his head, "You have much to learn from him."

Kekoa turned and walked to the fire pit, Konani was happy and smiling, and followed him. The holy man also walked to the fire pit, and sat down. Konani pulled a spirit ceremony plant from his basket, and showed it to the holy man.

"Thank you." The holy man said to the ancestors, "for this blessing."

"Are you hungry?" Konani asked Kekoa.

"Yes!" he said, "my belly wants fish!"

"We have caught many!" Konani said, and looked at me. He had waked me from sleep, to fish when the sun first lit the sky.

Kekoa laughed, and looked at the holy man, "He is trained well!"


"I HAVE NOT SEEN a man big like this," I told Konani, as we walked to the river, where the fish were held in a basket under the water.

"His sons are also big." Konani said.

"Has he taught you to fight as a warrior?" I asked.

Konani shook his head, "No, I will go to his village to learn this."

"You will be a warrior?"

"No, the holy man said we will learn to protect our self."

Konani pulled up the basket with fish in it, and shook his head.

"He will eat them all!" he told me.

I looked at Konani.

"Kekoa eats like no other man!" he said and laughed.

We started to walk back to camp.

"Kekoa will also teach us to travel on long boats."

"To fish?"

"No, we will train to travel."

I shook my head, I thought of the assistants that went to other islands.

"I do not want to go."

Konani nodded, "I do not want to go, yet I will be prepared."


THE HOLY MAN had started the fire, and he and Kekoa sat by it. Kekoa held a straight stick as long as his arm, with the branches taken off and the wood rubbed smooth. He also held the tip of another stick into the fire, then burned black marks on the smooth one.

"He is making a fighting stick." Konani said.

I watched Kekoa work. He burned black marks around the smooth wood, like the marks on his arms.

"I will teach you this." Kekoa said, and did not look up.


AFTER KONANI PREPARED THE FISH, the holy man put them on the fire.

"Bring fruits and plants." he told us.

Konani and I walked to the food hut, and I started to grab green leaves with my hands.

"Bring the basket." he told me.

I threw the leaves back in the basket, and picked it up. He picked up a basket with fruit, and we returned to the fire pit. When the fish was cooked, the holy man put leaves on a palm leaf, then fish, and more leaves over the fish. He handed the first palm leaf to Kekoa, and Kekoa nodded his head. The holy man gave Konani and me fish, then sat down by Kekoa. We waited for the holy man to speak, and I felt the palm leaf hot on my legs.

"Thank you for this fish," the holy man said, and looked at Kekoa, "Enjoy!"

We ate the fish, and the leaves that were hot and soft around it.

"Good!" Kekoa said, and put more into his mouth.

I watched Kekoa eat many more fish, and when all the fish was eaten, Konani gave fruit from his basket to Kekoa, and the holy man. He put the basket down by us, and we picked up fruit to eat. Kekoa told us of his family, we laughed much, and enjoyed tea.

"You make good fish!" Kekoa told the holy man.

The holy man smiled, "I like to watch you eat!"

"I am happy to eat for you!" Kekoa said, and laughed loudly.

Konani, the holy man, and I also laughed.

The holy man looked at Konani, "Clean."

Konani and I jumped up to clean, and I saw Kekoa lean close to the holy man, and speak quietly.

WITH DARKNESS ALL AROUND US, the flames rose up brightly from the fire pit. Konani and I finished cleaning and sat down. I saw Kekoa nodding his head, as the holy man spoke to him. I did not hear what he said, yet they were not laughing now. The holy man stopped talking, sat up straight, and Kekoa leaned back to sit. The holy man started to breath in, and out slowly. Kekoa closed his eyes, and Konani and I started to breath in and out like the holy man. I listened to the popping from the fire pit, as I breathed.

"Thank you ancestors for all you have given us." the holy man said.

I looked at Kekoa, and his eyes were shut.

"Thank you for being with us." the holy man said.

I looked into the darkness beyond the fire pit, and saw the light shadows of men.

"We ask you to guide Kekoa."

Now Kekoa opened his eyes, looking into the darkness, and I wondered if he also saw the ancestors. We did not move, as the holy man listened to the ancestors, then the holy man spoke.

"When the chief passes, his son will take the village down a bad path, and there will be much sadness."

"Can I help?" Kekoa asked.

"You will leave the village," the holy man said, "you will take your family in a boat under a big moon."

Kekoa nodded, and his eyes looked sad.

The holy man opened his eyes, and looked at Kekoa. "The ancestors guide you."

"Thank you." Kekoa said quietly.

"What do you see for the village?" the holy man asked.

Kekoa shook his head, "When the chief passes, his son will take his young warriors to fight all the villages on this island."

My eyes opened wide, "Battles on this island?"

"He wants to be chief of all the villages." Kekoa said.

The holy man looked at Kekoa, "He wants you to fight for him."

"This young bird spreads his wings, and stamps his feet" Kekoa said, and laughed.

"Be careful," the holy man said, "this young war bird will attack you."

Kekoa nodded, "I have seen young men such as this on my old island. I will take my family, and tell no one when I leave."

"Konani will go with you to your village," the holy man said, "when you to leave, send Konani to me."

"Yes" Kekoa said, "Konani will tell you of my travel."

The plan was made. Konani will go with Kekoa to his village, to be taught as other assistants had, and return when Kekoa left the village.

"When the sun rises," the holy man said, "I will take Konani for the medicine man ceremony, then he will leave with you."

Kekoa nodded his head.

"Your family will be safe." the holy man told Kekoa, "the ancestors travel with you."

Kekoa stood, and the holy man stood also.

Kekoa looked into the holy man's face, "I wanted peace, I wanted to watch my grandchildren grow."

"You will have this," the holy man said, "in a new village."

Kekoa put his big hand on the holy man's shoulder, "Thank you."

"Sleep well." the holy man told him.

Kekoa walked away to his hut, and the holy man walked to Konani. He leaned in, spoke into his ear, and Konani nodded.

"Thank you." Konani told the holy man.

Then the holy man walked to his hut, and Konani waved for me to come with him, to our hut.

"What is the ceremony?" I asked Konani.

"I will see my teacher." Konani said.

"Will you eat the plant you found?"

"No, that is for the mountain village."

"What will the holy man do?"

"He will open the fires in my body."

"Fires?"

"The light from the sun," he said, "will come through me for healing."

I did not know what Konani spoke of.

He put his hands out, "My hands will get hot from this."

I thought of when the holy man rested his hands on my shoulders at the river. "The holy man's hands were hot when he blessed me."

Konani nodded, "I will be a medicine man after the ceremony."

We walked into the hut, and Konani sat on his mat.

"Will you also be a holy man?" I asked.

"No," Konani smiled, "that comes after I have learned much more."

"Oh," I said, and sat down on my mat.

"I feel we will not stay here long." he told me.

"Where will we go?" I asked, "I left my village to come here!"

"The ancestors guide the holy man," Konani said, "he will take care of you."

I took in a deep breath and blew it out. Konani stretched out on his mat, and turned his back to me. I laid down on my mat, and looked up.

"Ancestors protect me." I closed my eyes, and saw the ancestors with the feather head dresses.

"We are with you." I heard, as sleep came to me.

# CHAPTER 4

*I* awoke, and it was still dark in the hut. I looked across to see Konani sleeping, I heard birds, and knew the sun would be up soon. I grabbed my sandals, and walked quietly out of the hut. Looking over to the fire pit, I saw a large shadow of a man sitting, and knew it was Kekoa. I went to stand by Kekoa, and watched him poke a stick into the fire pit. He pushed dirt from some burned wood, found where it was still hot, then threw dry leaves on it to make small flames.

"How long have you been here?" Kekoa asked me.

"Not long."

He began to throw small branches on the fire, and the flames grew bigger.

"Learn quickly from the holy man." Kekoa said, and turned to look in my eyes.

"This peace will end soon."

"Will there be battles?" I asked.

Kekoa turned his head to look at the fire, and did not speak. I watched him, and waited.

"Listen to the holy man," he said, "you will be safe."

"I will."

. . .

I WATCHED THE FIRE, then thought, "Konani is leaving! I must bring the food, and make the tea!"

I grabbed the tea pot, which was full of fresh water, and placed it near the fire. Kekoa watched me, threw more branches around the pot, and soon the flames heated the water.

The moon still traveled in the sky, yet sun light began to come through the trees. I walked to the food hut, opened the door, and grabbed baskets with fresh fruit, dried fish, and nuts. I wanted Kekoa to fill his belly. I grabbed some torn palm leaves to hold the food, then backed out of the hut, and closed the door. When I turned around, I saw the holy man talking to Kekoa and Konani.

"Did you get tea leaves?" Konani asked.

"No." I answered.

"Good, the holy man wants to make his tea this morning."

I put the basket down next to the holy man.

Kekoa looked at me, and nodded.

The holy man rose from his seat, walked into his hut, returning with a handful of leaves that he put into the tea pot. After everyone finished eating, we sipped our tea.

"This tea is strong," Kekoa said, "I like it!"

The holy man smiled, "These leaves are from the mountain."

I sipped the hot tea, and also liked it.

"I will take Konani for the ancestors to bless," the holy man said, and looked at me.

"Take Kekoa to the food hut, and he will get food to travel."

"We will leave when you return." Kekoa told the holy man.

"Kai," Konani said, "you will clean this day."

I nodded, and watched the holy man and Konani walk to the holy man's hut. The holy man stepped into his hut, and came out with the basket he used for blessing villages.

The holy man and Konani walked away, and I turned around to the fire pit and Kekoa.

I quickly cleaned, while Kekoa drank tea. I carried the hot tea pot with a palm leaf, and walked to the river. Squatting down, I emptied the leaves into the pool of water, then added fresh water from where the river spilled into the pool. Looking up, I saw Kekoa walking to the me. He climbed over a rock, and got into the water. Kekoa's head went under the water, and when he came up, he spit water up in the air and laughed.

"I like to swim in river water" he said, and went back under the water kicking his feet as he did.

"Will the chief's son attack villages?" I asked, when Kekoa got out of the water.

"Yes," he said, "he will fight village elders to be the chief."

"Fight the elders?"

"I left my home island after such a battle." he said, and shook his head.

"My family was killed, and I was wounded." Kekoa looked down, "We were fishermen, and not prepared to fight against the men that wanted our village."

"The villages must prepare." I told him, not wanting my family killed.

"Yes," Kekoa said, and looked at me. "I learned to fight after I healed, and became a warrior."

"I will learn also."

Kekoa put his hand on my shoulder, "You are yet small, and cannot fight."

I bit my lip, and felt water come into my eyes.

"The holy man will protect you." Kekoa said.

"My family?" I asked, and looked at him.

"The villages will be warned, so they can prepare."

"I want to help them!" I said, not knowing how I would do this.

"You are a good boy." Kekoa said, and squeezed my shoulder. Then he let go, and walked back to the fire pit. I stood, looking across the river, at the dark water passing by.

"A boy!" I thought, "I am not a man, I cannot protect myself, or my family!"

When I left my village, I was happy. I traveled far from my mother, yet I knew I would learn many new things, and be trained to make medicine. Now, the things that I have learned, have brought me fear.

"I am not ready." I thought, "I want to be with my family."

"Do not fear." a voice said.

I looked around, yet knew this was an ancestor.

"You were guided to be here now."

My body felt heavy, and my arms hung down at my sides. I took in a deep breath and blew it out.

"I will stay, yet I do not want to!"


KONANI TURNED TO WAVE, as he followed Kekoa down the trail, out of camp. I watched, and when I could no longer see Konani, I walked over to join the holy man at the fire pit.

"We will prepare. " the holy man said, "we will gather plants, dry them, and make medicine."

I nodded.

"I will teach you quickly," he said, "we will make many medicines."

He was quiet, I watched him think, then he looked at me.

"When Konani returns, we will leave, and take our medicine to the villages."

"We will tell them of the chief's son?" I asked.

"Yes," he said, "are you ready?"

I nodded, "I am ready."


EACH MORNING, after eating, we held large baskets in each hand, water pouches that I filled in the river, and walked out of camp to gather plants. The holy man told me when to pick only the leaves, and when I would pull the plant from the dirt. He showed me berries that we did not eat, yet were used in medicine, he showed me tree barks and many other plants.

From the river, we scraped soft plants from the rocks under the water, and scooped out tiny fish, which we dried for medicine. The holy man showed me how to use mud and plants to dry poison from wounds, then which plants to use after the wound was dry. There were plants for cuts, for pain, for women, and for making the sick strong again. I listened carefully to what he told me, and found I liked making medicines.

I had seen mother use mud on wounds, and make berry tea for me when I was sick, yet I had not seen this many medicines. I wanted to learn how to use every plant on the island.

"You are good at learning medicine." the holy man said.

"I like it." I told him.


AFTER FILLING OUR BASKETS, we returned to camp, and laid plants on rocks to dry in the sun. We hung dried plants in the hut, then ate and rested. We made many medicines to put in the food hut. The holy man had large and small pouches to carry medicine, and he taught me to make them. I also learned of the leaves the holy man put on our fish, some were dried, and some freshly picked.


WE WORKED QUIETLY, with the holy man showing me how to grind each plant. Some plants needed to be ground into powder, while other plants must be broken with a blade. Some plants were mixed together in the camp, and other plants would be mixed before using.

The holy man told me of each plant, and how it was used. He warned me that some plants could be poison if too much are used, and that there are plants I must not put my hands on. I must cover my hands, use leaves or a blade, to prepare it.

"When will I know all the plants?"

The holy man laughed, "I have not learned all the plants can teach us!"

"I find many new ways to use them, as you will also." he told me.

In my mind, I saw myself as a grown man, gathering plants and making medicines, yet I did not know the island. The island was larger, and there were plants I had not seen.

"Have I seen all the plants on this island?" I asked.

"Not all, but most that we use for medicine."

OUR FOOD HUT stored more medicine than food. The holy man and I picked fruit each day while we gathered plants, and ate them as we worked. We fished when we returned to camp, and only kept dried fruit and fish in the hut now.

"When we travel, we will carry the dried fruit, fish and our medicines. We will have our bedroll and water pouch, yet we will travel fast." the holy man told me.

As we drank our tea at the fire pit, the holy man sat quietly looking at me.

"You must be strong." he said.

I looked at him, not knowing why he said this.

"You will carry my baskets, and yours. You will swim each day," he told me.

I knew the holy man wanted to help me, so I nodded, "I will do this."

NOW BEFORE LEAVING to pick plants, the holy man strapped a large basket on my back, and gave me large baskets to hold in each hand. I followed him, as he gathered plants, and put them in the baskets I carried. I also gathered plants, and carried my plants as well. We picked fruit to dry, and put those in the baskets. Soon the baskets were heavy, and I walked slower.

"Keep walking." the holy man told me.

He put more fruit into the baskets I carried, and my feet were getting hard to lift from the ground.

The holy man pointed toward camp, "We go back," and walked in front of me.

I followed, with each step I felt my shoulders and back hurt, and my arms pulled down to carry the baskets. I walked slowly, and returned to camp far behind the holy man. When I walked into camp, he came to me, and lifted the basket from my back.

"Go swim." he told me.

I ran to the water, and jumped into the deep pool. The water felt good on my body. The holy man joined me in the water, swimming in the pool, then he climbed out to lay on a rock in the sun. I started to follow him, and he spoke,

"You must swim to that rock", he pointed to a rock just before the river ran hard to the waterfall, "then swim back. Do this again and again. When your body is tired, and you cannot swim, then climb out."

I looked at the rock, and began swimming. I reached the rock, then swam back. I turned and swam to the rock, then back. I turned again, and as I swam to the rock, my arms and legs felt tired. I rested at the rock and swam back again, my body wanted to stop, and I thought of climbing out of the water.

"Swim." the holy man said.

"I am tired," I told him.

He sat up, and pointed back to the rock.

I took a breath in and blew it out, then started swimming back to the rock. My body felt heavy, and I swam slowly, yet I reached the rock. I looked back at the holy man, and he nodded, then I swam back to him.

"Good," he said, "do this each day after we gather plants."

Many big moons passed, and I could now carry heavy baskets, and swim many times to the rock and back. I had also learned how to make many medicines.

"You have grown." the holy man said looking at me, and nodded, "you are stronger."

This made me happy, and I knew that when we traveled on the trails, I would carry my own basket and walk fast with the holy man and Konani.

DARKNESS FELL ON THE CAMP, I sat with the holy man, and watched fish cook over the fire. We had worked long this day, my body was tired, and my stomach was hungry. This day I had learned to weave a large medicine basket, and we spoke of that.

"Do I use the same plant to weave both the small and large medicine baskets?" I asked.

"There are," suddenly the holy man stopped talking, and listened, "Go into your hut, and do not come out."

He pointed to my hut. I jumped up, and ran into my hut, stopping just inside the door to look out. I heard it also, someone was coming up the trail. I heard the rocks under running feet, and the sound of hard breathing. Then a dark shadow showed behind the fire pit, and walked closer to the holy man. The fire light shown on legs, and I looked up to see the face.

"Konani!" It was Konani!

I ran out of the hut, and to the fire pit "Konani!" I called out.

"Kai," he looked at me, "you have grown!"

"Sit" the holy man said, "We will eat, and you will tell us of Kekoa."

"Yes." Konani said.

The holy man put the hot fish on palm leaves, and gave it to us.

Konani ate quickly, "This is good!"

I watched Konani as I ate, and when he finished, I took his palm leaf and grabbed the pot of tea from the fire pit.

"The old chief lay in his hut when Kekoa and I returned." Konani said, "villagers came to him each day."

"He was preparing to pass." the holy man said.

Konani nodded, "Yet his son did not stay with him."

The holy man shook his head, "The old chief had much to teach him."

"His son prepared to fight. He stayed on the sand, training with his young warriors."

"Did Kekoa train you?" the holy man asked.

Konani nodded, "He taught me much."

"Good." the holy man said.

"I learned to track, learned to travel and not leave my marks on the trail. I learned to sleep as the animals, and not be found."

"Did you learn to fight?" I asked.

"Yes," he said, "Kekoa showed me how to fight, and throw spears."

The holy man nodded, and I leaned forward, listening carefully to what he said.

"He taught me to use my travel stick as a weapon." and picked up his stick to pound on the dirt.

"Each day Kekoa trained me, as he had trained other young men. The chief's son thought Kekoa did this, so that I would fight with them. He did not know, we would leave when his father passed.

The chief's son sat at the fire pit each night, and spoke loudly of being chief of all the villages. He spoke of joining with women in each village, so that he would have many children."

Konani stopped to look at me. My eyes were open wide, as I looked back.

"He will attack the villages, and take the village boys to be his warriors."

"He said this?" the holy man asked.

Konani nodded.

"The ancestors told me of this," the holy man said.

"These young warriors want to fight, and take what they want from the villagers."

"Will their village elders not stop them?" I asked.

Konani shook his head, "Kekoa has told them of the battles on his home island, and of many villagers that passed, yet the chief's son and his men do not hear his words."

The holy man shook his head.

"The elders have spoken against this also, yet there are many warriors, and they do not listen to their fathers or grandfathers."

"The chief has passed." the holy man said.

"Yes, his passing ceremony was under the big moon." Konani said.

I looked up, and saw the moon was still big.

"What of Kekoa?" the holy man asked.

"After the ceremony we went to his hut, and he told me and his family we would wait for the village to sleep, then leave. He took them on a boat, and I ran up the trail."

The holy man looked at the moon. "It is a good night to travel."

I thought of leaving on a boat in the darkness, and was glad I did not travel with Kekoa.

"Kekoa said he would travel along the island to his woman's village, and wait for you. The young warriors know he will warn the villages, and will come after him when they find he has left."

The holy man took a big breath and blew it out, " It has started. We will call the ancestors to guide us."

The holy man, Konani and I sat quietly breathing in and breathing out. I felt someone standing behind me.

"Kai" the holy man said, "your grandfather stands by you."

"I felt him." I told him.

"He will guide you when I am not here."

I looked at him, and did not know why he said this.

"Your grandfather will hear your thoughts," the holy man said, "speak to him, and know he will be with you."

"Thank you" I said.

"I will wake you when it is dark," the holy man told me, "we will pack our baskets full of medicines."

Konani nodded.

"We will drink the mountain tea and leave, and we will not stop." the holy man said.

"Kai," he said, "Fill the water pouches now. We will travel fast, and see Kekoa at the village, before the chief's son and his men get there."

My heart pounded, and I nodded to him. I cleaned, got fresh water for morning tea and filled the pouches, while Konani and the holy man talked quietly. When I returned from the river, they stopped talking and looked at me.

"Sit" the holy man said.

I sat, and looked at their faces. They did not smile.

"You have learned much," the holy man told me, "and know the medicines now.

"You have grown, and are stronger." Konani said.

The holy man looked at Konani, then turned back to me

"You must be a medicine man." the holy man looked into my eyes, "we will leave the camp, and you will walk as a man, no longer a boy."

I did not speak.

"I will take you for the ceremony," the holy man told me, "after that, you will be a medicine man."

"Man?" I asked.

"Yes, you will give medicines, and be guided by your teacher."

I looked at them, with many thoughts in my head.

"The ancestors tell me to give you the ceremony."

I looked at Konani.

"There are stories of another young medicine man." Konani said.

"I knew him when he was an old man," the holy man said, "he told me his teacher was ready to pass, and gave him the ceremony when he was a boy."

"Have I learned..." I started to ask.

"You have much to learn, yet you will learn this as you grow."

I looked at Konani.

"I will teach you what Kekoa showed me." Konani said.

I took in a big breath, and thought of what they told me.

"We sleep." the holy man said, and stood up. He stepped to me, and put his hand on my shoulder.

"I will wake you."


Konani and I went into our hut, Konani laid down on his bed, and soon slept. I turned from side to side, then lay on my back, and looked up. Many thoughts filled my head. I lay there thinking of the ceremony, and thinking of chief's son, and his warriors.

"We must arrive at the village before the chief's son." I thought.

My body was tired, yet my mind would not sleep. Then I felt a hand on my shoulder, and I turned quickly, to see if the holy man stood there. The hut was empty and dark, only Konani lay asleep on his mat.

"Oh" I thought, it must be my grandfather.

"Help me sleep" I whispered.

"Close your eyes" I heard in my mind.

I closed my eyes, and the thoughts began to go away. I breathed slowly, saw only darkness, then I saw no more.

I AWOKE to the holy man shaking my shoulder. He put his finger up to his mouth, and walked quietly from our hut. I sat up, grabbed my sandals, and followed him out. It was dark, with small streaks of light coming through the trees. I put on my sandals, and saw he had his ceremony pouch with him. He put a stick with reed wrapped around the end, into the fire pit. The hot wood at the bottom of the fire pit, made the reed burn, and the holy man held it up in front of him.

"Come."

I followed the holy man and listened to the birds. The air was cool, I held my arms across my chest, and my legs felt cold. The holy man walked off the path, and through bushes toward the mountain. I had not traveled here, and looked ahead to see where we went.

"Here." the holy man said.

I looked at a small pool of water, with many flowers growing around it. Soft plants grew over the rocks next to the water, which was very still.

"This is the ceremony place of the ancestors." he pointed to a rock, that stood high, and was flat across the top. The holy man opened his ceremony pouch, and placed what was inside, on top of the flat rock. A feather, a bundle of dried plant tied with string, a half shell, and a large rock with clear spears coming out from it.

"Sit." He told me, and pointed beside the ceremony rock.

I sat down with my legs crossed. He took the bundle of dried plant, and lit it with the fire from the stick he carried. He laid the stick down on the dirt, where it began to burn out. The holy man blew on the bound dried plant, until smoke rose in the air. He held the dried plant in one hand, grabbed the large feather with the other hand, and waved the smoke from the plant around me.

"We ask the ancestors to join us for this ceremony. We ask for Kai's ancestor teacher to be here this day."

The holy man walked slowly around me, pushing the smoke with the feather, until I could smell the smoke all around my head.

"We ask our ancestors to protect Kai, and to guide his hands when he makes medicine. We ask the ancestors to guide him when he speaks to the villagers. We ask the ancestors to speak to Kai, and tell him what he must know."

I listened carefully, and wanted to hear all the holy man said.

"We ask the ancestors to walk with us, until we pass to join with them."

The holy man walked to the pool of water, waved the feather and smoke over it, and around the rocks. He turned to the flat rock, and put the feather and smoking plant down, then he picked up the half shell. He filled it with water from the pool, and laid the shell back on the ceremony rock.

"We offer our ancestors water."

The holy man picked up the rock with spears, and placed it next to the water. A stream of light shone down through the trees onto the rock, and my mouth fell open, as the rock lit up like the sun and shined light out from the spears. The holy man closed his eyes, and held his hands over the clear rock, and his lips moved, yet I did not hear his words. Then the holy man opened his eyes, and walked to me, placing his hands on my shoulders. His hands felt hot on me.

"Close your eyes, and breath quietly" he said.

I closed my eyes, and felt the heat from his hands pass into my shoulders. It was hot, as it traveled from my shoulders down my back to where I sat, and all my body felt like I sat next to a large fire. My face burned, I took in a deep breath, then a feeling of peace came around me. The holy man put his hands over my ears.

"Ancestors, let Kai hear you." he said.

Suddenly I felt pain in my ears, then I heard a loud sound. I shook my head, and the holy man dropped his hands, and put them on my shoulders. I sat, not moving under the holy man's hands, then the pain and sound left my ears. The holy man put his hands on top of my head, and I felt the heat again.

"Ancestors, let Kai know what you show him."

I felt the heat travel from my head down into my body. The holy man moved his hands, and pressed his fingers into my forehead, between my eyebrows. My eyes were closed, yet I saw light inside my head. Then he held his hands on the sides of my head, and I felt them shake.

"With the ancestors' blessing, Kai is now a medicine man, and will join our circle of medicine men . Thank you ancestors, thank you Father, thank you Mother."

I heard him take in a big breath and blow it out, then he lifted his hands, and I felt water from the shell slowly pour on my head. My hair was wet, water ran down my face, and dripped onto my chest and back.

"Come here." the holy man said, and stepped to the pool of water.

I walked to stand beside him, then he squatted down, and made ripples in the water with his hand.

"Look into the water." he said, and stepped back away from me.

I looked at the water, and saw ripples traveling across to the other side. I watched as they went away, and the water stood still and clear again. I saw myself in the water, and kneeled down to look at my face. Suddenly a face next to mine looked back at me. I was surprised, and looked around, yet only the holy man stood back next to a tree.

I turned back to the water, and saw this face now smiling at me. It was a beautiful face. I heard a voice in my head, "I am with you." then the face went away and I saw only myself. I stood up, and turned to the holy man.

"She is a woman!" I called to him, "my teacher is a woman!"

# CHAPTER 5

We gathered fresh fruit as we walked back to camp, Konani had the tea pot in the fire pit, and baskets filled with medicines and food. He looked at us and smiled, then walked to me, and grabbed my arm,

"Welcome." he said.

I looked at him, and my chest felt warm. "He is my brother." I thought.

I looked at the holy man, and my chest warmed again, "He is also my brother."

I knew that we were all brothers in the circle of medicine men.

"The ceremony has done this." I heard my teacher say.

We drank the mountain tea, ate the fresh fruit, and I was ready to travel. The holy man unrolled my bedroll, and hung the blanket over my shoulders to cover my back, then strapped a basket heavy with medicines on me.

"If it slows you," he told me, "we will carry it."

I tied my bed roll back together, and slipped the strap over my shoulder. The holy man had woven straps to our water pouches, and we put those over our shoulders also. We carried a small basket with dried fish, fruit, and plants in our hands. Konani put rocks on the fire, then threw dirt on them, until no smoke came from it. The holy man walked to his hut and looked inside, then came out, and looked over the camp.

"We thank you ancestors for this camp. We thank you Father and Mother for giving us food and water, and this good day to travel. We ask you to protect and guide us."

Konani and I watched him bend down, and grab dirt in his hands. He closed his eyes, spoke quietly, then walked to the fire pit and threw it in. Then he walked to the river, squatted down, and washed his hands and face. He stood and looked at the river, then turned to walk back.

"Are you ready?"

We nodded our heads.

"Good." the holy man said, then turned and walked to the trail by the waterfall, and out of our camp.

I followed and looked at the water which sparkled as I had not seen before, the colors of the sky and plants were also bright and beautiful. I wondered if the ceremony had made me see in a new way.

"Did the heat in the holy man's hands," I thought, "make my eyes see more clearly?"

I thought of my teacher's face, "Thank you for being with me."

At the waterfall, the holy man took the basket from my back, and hand.

"Follow Konani." he said.

Konani climbed down ahead of me, and I carefully stepped where he did, holding tight to branches along the way. I looked away from my feet, over to the waterfall, and suddenly my foot slipped. I felt the branch pull from my hand and I fell down, sliding on my legs.

Konani turned and yelled, "Grab the bush!"

I reached over with both hands and grabbed a bush, feeling it tear at my skin, as I held tight and stopped moving. I turned, and looked up to see the holy man, carrying my baskets as he climbed down.

"Look where you walk!" the holy man said. Then he reached me, and helped me stand.

"Are you hurt?"

I looked at my hands, and saw cuts with red water. "I can travel." I told him.

He looked at my hands, and shook his head.

Konani stood at the bottom, watching us.

"Follow me." the holy man said, and climbed down ahead of me.

I carefully climbed behind him, and did not look away from my feet, until I stood on the trail at the bottom.

"Let me see your hands." Konani said, and grabbed them. He looked at them, then poured water from his pouch on the cuts.

The holy man put the medicine basket on my back, gave me the little basket, and walked quickly away.

"Walk fast." Konani told me, and turned to follow the holy man.

I lifted the straps on my shoulders, then let them come down again.

"I am ready." I told myself, and began to walk quickly behind Konani.


WE TRAVELED, and did not stop. I felt the back of my legs hurt, and knew they must also have cuts, yet I kept walking.

"I will carry my basket," I thought, "and I will travel fast."

I watched Konani as I walked.

"I am a medicine man." The holy man had taught me about plants, and how to make medicines.

"I fish, I make tea, and I clean." I thought of when I slept in my mother's hut, on a mat with my brothers.

"I sleep on my own mat," I thought, "I am not a boy."

When I left my village, I did not know where I would travel, or what I would do. I did not know how I would grow, and be strong now.

"I have traveled, and seen new villages. I have learned of the ancestors, and know my teacher is with me."

I smiled, "I do not need my mother to care for me."

"Kai!" Konani called, "Is the basket heavy?"

"I will carry it." I answered, thinking how I could not carry my own bed roll, when I last walked on this trail.

"I am strong!" I yelled.

"Good" Konani said, and I heard him laugh.

MY BELLY WAS HUNGRY, so I pulled a dried fish from the basket I carried. I saw Konani eating as he walked also. The trail was no longer shaded by the trees, and the sun shined down on us. Water ran down from my hair, and my face was hot. My back was wet under the blanket and basket, and my legs hurt where water ran into the cuts. I drank from my pouch, and poured a little on my face.

"I will not stop." I told myself.

I knew the trail was leading back to the sea, and the village where we would see Kekoa. I thought of the young girl, Milana, and wondered if I would see her. Then I wondered what would happen when the chief's son came into her village.

"How will they protect her?" I thought, and suddenly knew why we carried heavy baskets with medicine.

"It is for the battle wounds!" I thought, and saw Kekoa's long battle wound in my head.

"How can I help them? I have not learned this!" My heart felt heavy.

"Do not think of this now." I heard my teacher say.

I looked ahead at Konani, then the holy man in front of him.

"The ancestors have guided them," I thought, and was glad they also led me.

They told the holy man to teach me medicine, they gave me the ceremony so I could see my teacher, and made the holy man and Konani my brothers in the circle of medicine men. I thought of when the holy man asked a boy to leave his family, and now I returned as a medicine man.

"Walk faster." I heard the holy man call back.

Then he started walking faster, making noises as he walked under the weight of his large basket. He had packed his basket past the top, and held the medicine down with a mat and woven straps. Konani also walked faster, and I stretched my legs as far as I could, to stay behind them. I felt the basket pulling down on my shoulders, and swinging from side to side. It rubbed my bare skin, where the blanket had fallen away under the basket, yet I did not slow down.

THE TRAIL WENT DOWN, and my legs now hurt in front also. My back burned where the basket fell against it, and rubbed it's weight on me. I saw Konani getting further ahead of me, and I tried to walk fast, yet my legs were shaking with each step. I saw Konani follow the trail around the mountain, and I stopped pushing my legs to walk as fast. I slowed, yet kept walking. Finally, I reached where the trail turned, and saw Konani had stopped.

"Look." he said, and pointed to the water by the village.

The holy man had not stopped, and was far ahead.

Konani turned, began to walk, and I followed. The trail was narrow here, and we were careful to watch where we stepped. Konani walked slower, and I was glad. My legs and back hurt, yet I could stay behind him. I started to feel the air that blew from the sea, and I smelled the water. A sea bird flew over our heads, and cried loudly to us. I thought of taking my basket off, and sitting on the sand.

"I will swim when we get to the village." I told Konani.

"I will also!" he called back.

THE TRAIL REACHED the bottom of the mountain, and we walked under trees. I was glad to walk in the shade, and feel the cool wind. I saw a hut under a tree by the trail, and we soon walked past it, and waved to women working there. We passed more huts, and more villagers on both sides of the trail, then we saw the waves ahead, and men standing around the fire pit.

"I see Kekoa!" Konani yelled, and I was happy that he was here.

We walked to the fire pit, and saw the holy man next to Kekoa.

"Welcome!" called Kekoa, walked to Konani, and slapped his arm.

Then he looked at me, and called out loudly, "Welcome!"

Konani and I both smiled, and pulled at our baskets. Konani dropped his to the sand.

"I heard your belly!" Konani said, and laughed.

I laughed, "I am hungry."

I pulled at the blanket, which stuck to my back. Konani lifted it from my shoulders.

"You need medicine," he told me, "the basket has rubbed your skin off."

There was pain where he pulled the blanket from me. A woman brought us water to drink, and Konani poured some of it on my wound, then we sat on logs by the holy man. Kekoa and the holy man spoke to the men of the village. Another woman brought us a palm leaf with fresh fruit, a fish was taken from the fire pit, and given to us.

"Thank you." I said when she handed it to me.

I was happy to eat, and looked at Konani who already had a mouth full of fruit. As I ate, I looked for Milana in the village, yet did not see her.

Konani stood, and rubbed his belly. "My belly is happy."

I stood, and rubbed mine, "Do you want to swim?"

The holy man looked at Konani, "Give medicine."

Then he looked at me, "Go with Konani."

Kekoa now looked at us, "The chief's son will come soon."

"I will put medicine on your back, then we will see the villagers." Konani said.

He mixed water with ground leaves and patted it on my wound.

"Leave your basket here," Konani told me, and we walked into the village.

I followed Konani to women working by a hut.

"Do you need medicine?" he asked the women.

"My father is old, and lays in his hut." a woman told him.

"Show me." Konani said.

We followed the woman to a small hut where her father lay on his

59

mat. He was small, with the bones of his face and neck just under his skin. His knees were bent, and the leg bones held no fat on them. The old man smiled at us.

"Do you need medicine?" Konani asked.

"I am old, your medicine will not help," he said, "sit and tell me of your travels."

Konani sat on the floor next to him, and I sat next to Konani.

"My name is Konani, this is Kai. We are medicine men, and travel with the holy man."

"You are medicine men?" the old man said, and looked at me.

"He has taught us medicine." Konani told him.

"This is good." the holy man nodded, and smiled, "I was young when my father taught me to fish."

Konani told him of our camp, and how we gather plants to make medicine. I wondered why we sat here, when the old man did not want medicine, and we had not seen other villagers. Konani was happy to sit, and speak with the old man. The old man and Konani laughed many times, and the old man told us many things of when he was young. I moved to put my legs under me, and Konani turned to look at me.

"Ready to go?" Konani asked.

"Yes," I said, and looked at the old man, "we will see other villagers."

"Yes, " Konani turned to the old man, "we will leave, when the sun rises I will return."

"Good." the old man said with a big smile, "Good."

We stood, and walked out of the hut.

"He did not need medicine," I said, "yet you stayed to talk with him."

"I gave him medicine" Konani said.

I did not see Konani open his basket to get medicine, and I stopped to look at him.

"I did not see this."

"There are many medicines," Konani said, "the holy man taught me that giving good feelings, will heal just as giving medicine."

I was quiet, and looked at Konani.

"There is much you need to learn." he told me.

"Yes." I said, knowing I must watch Konani carefully, and learn from him.

WE WENT TO ANOTHER HUT, where a young woman and new baby, still lay. The young mother's skin was pale, and she was weak, yet the baby looked happy and drank from the mother's breast.

"I will give you medicine," Konani said, "to make you strong."

"Thank you" she said in a little voice.

Konani put his basket down and reached in, he grabbed fresh leaves, and a pouch with ground dried plants.

"Make tea with these" he said to a grandmother in the hut.

"Give her tea many times each day, it will make her strong. Also give her fish when the sun rises." Konani said strongly. The grandmother nodded her head, and took the medicine to make tea.

"You must drink the tea, and eat much." Konani told the young mother.

She nodded.

"I will return." Konani said.

I FOLLOWED Konani into another hut, where a child lay with hot skin, and to another where an old woman sat with sore bones. In each hut Konani gave medicine, and told them how to use it.

"The holy man has taught you much." I said.

"I am blessed."

I grabbed Konani's arm, "I want to learn from you."

"I will teach you." he said, and turned to walk back to the fire pit.

As we got closer to the group of men, we heard them speaking loudly.

"We cannot hide with women, children and the elders!" a man said.

"We cannot fight them!" another yelled.

Kekoa held his large hand up, and the men stopped talking,

"We will go to new island." Kekoa said, "it is not safe to stay."

Men began to shout, "Another island, where?' "Our boats cannot take all the village!"

Kekoa held up his hand again, "We will take the young men, women and children to another island. The chief's son will not want the old."

The men of the village looked at each other, "We will not leave our elders!"

A grandfather stood, and the men stopped speaking.

"My children and grandchildren will be safe," he said, "I will stay in the village."

Then another grandfather stood, "I will stay."

Then another stood, and another, each saying they would stay. The village chief stood, and looked around, I saw water in his eyes.

"The grandfathers and grandmothers will stay in the village," he said, "Kekoa will take our young to another island."

"We will leave when the sun rises." Kekoa told them.

"Will we fight the chief's son?" an old man said.

Kekoa turned to him, "No! Do not fight!"

"What will we do?" another asked.

Kekoa looked at the villagers as he thought, then he nodded his head, and spoke.

"Tell the warriors the young died with a great sickness."

The grandfathers listened carefully.

"The chief's son cannot fight sickness," Kekoa said, "he will leave."

"Yes!" the villagers called out, "This is good."

"The young that cannot travel will leave the village, and hide." Kekoa told them.

"There are sea caves," a man said, "they can hide there."

"I have traveled on the sea, and I know an island where we will make a new village." Kekoa said.

A grandmother started to cry loudly, and called out, "Will we not see our children again?"

Kekoa looked at her, "We will return for you."

The villagers now spoke to each other about preparing. Many men left the fire pit, to tell their families.

"Take only dried fish and fruit," he yelled, "and fresh water!"

I WATCHED THEM, and felt their sad hearts. The grandfathers would not watch their sons fish, or enjoy them at the fire pit. The grandmothers would see their children and grandchildren leave, and there would be no more babies to care for. My heart hurt, I wanted to sit on the sand, and look at the waves. I looked at Konani, and pointed to the sea.

"Go" he said.

I walked down to the water, and sat. Looking out over the waves to the flat sea, I wondered what it would be like, to get in a boat and go there. The sea was big, like the sky.

"I do not want to go on the boats." I thought, and in my mind saw myself under a night sky, in a boat, with the great dark water all around me. My shoulders shook, and I felt fear.

"Ancestors," I said, "guide them to a new island, and let them be safe."

I sat on the sand, with my arms wrapped around my bent legs, and watched the sun drop down into the sea. I looked far out across the water, and saw it was clear. That was good for the travelers that would leave soon. I thought of this village, and the families being torn apart, by sending the young away. Some grandfathers and grandmothers would pass before their families would return, and they would not know if their children arrived safely at the new island.

My heart hurt for this village, and I wondered what my village would do. Would they also send families away? Would there be fighting? Battles like those that gave Kekoa his wounds? Kekoa would not be with them to guide them to a new island. What would my father and brothers do to protect our family?

DARKNESS FELL, and I looked up at the lights in the sky. I heard the waves pushing up on the sand, and I stood to walk to it. I put my foot in the water, and it felt good.

"I did not swim." I thought.

I turned to walk back, and saw a dark shadow on the sand. It looked like a piece of wood left by the sea, yet it moved.

"Milana!" I called, and walked to her.

"Milana." I said again.

She did not turn her head to look at me, and did not speak.

"I will watch the sky with you."

She lay quiet, yet I saw her put a hand to her eye. I lay down on the sand, with my arms behind my head, and looked up.

I was closer to the village now, and heard many sounds coming from huts. Villagers speaking loudly, and cries, not only of babies, there were cries of mothers.

"Will you leave?" I asked her.

"Yes" her little voice said.

"I am sad you must leave your village." I told her.

"I," she started to speak, her voice cracked, and she said no more.

I saw Milana lay her arm across her face, I heard her make small sounds, and I knew water fell from her eyes.

"I will leave my grandfather!" she said.

"Only the young will travel" I told her.

"He can travel!" she cried.

I looked at her, "He is old?"

She was quiet, and rubbed water from her face.

"My mother and father passed when I was little, my grandfather has cared for me."

"Where is your grandmother?"

"She passed when my mother came, and grandfather did not join with a new woman."

"Oh." I said, thinking on this.

"I have only my grandfather," she said quietly, "I do not want to leave him."

I felt a hand on my shoulder, and my teacher whispered in my ear, "She will see her grandfather again."

"My teacher has told me," I said, "you will see your grandfather again."

Milana sat up, and looked at me, "When?"

I looked out over the sea, and in my mind, saw boats coming in to the sand. A young woman, with long hair, helped pull the boat in. I knew this was Milana, as a woman, returning to the village.

"You will be a woman, and will return with others." I told her.

"A woman?" she said, "yet my grandfather has not passed?"

"He will not."

She looked to the sea, and nodded her head. "Good."

Then she looked back at me, "The holy man has taught you to speak with the ancestors?"

"Yes."

"I want the holy man to teach me." she said, "I want to speak with my mother."

"Your mother?"

"I feel her with me."

"She will travel with you to the new island." I told her.

"Good," she said, and stood up, "I will go to my grandfather now."

She was small, and I wondered how this girl would travel across the sea. She would leave her grandfather, and go to a new island, with no family. I jumped to my feet, and wrapped my arms around her.

"Travel well." I said.

Her arms hung down, and she leaned her head against my chest, "Thank you."

I dropped my arms, and she looked up at me.

"Will you go?" she asked.

"No, I will travel with the holy man, to warn my village."

"Travel well." she said, turned to walk away, then stopped and looked back at me,

"When I return, I will learn from the holy man."

I smiled, "I will speak to him."

She nodded and walked away.

I walked back to the fire pit, and saw the holy man and Kekoa speaking.

"My woman will leave, and she fears for her mother," Kekoa said, "yet my sons are happy to find a new island."

"I am glad," the holy man said, "you can guide the boats across the water."

Kekoa nodded.

"Our villages fish, we do not fight!" the holy man said.

"Yes," Kekoa said, "The villagers cannot win a battle."

Konani looked at me, "You have returned."

I sat on the log near him.

"I will go to my family." Kekoa stood, and reached over to slap Konani's shoulder.

"Will you go with me?" he asked.

Konani looked at the holy man, and back to Kekoa, "No."

Kekoa smiled, "I will return for you."

Konani nodded, and I saw water in his eyes. Kekoa walked away, and the holy man stood up. He rolled his shoulders, and moved his head around.

"We will sleep," he told us, then looked at me, "after Kekoa leaves, we go to your village."

Konani and I stood up, followed him to where our baskets and bed rolls lay by a palm tree.

"I am tired." Konani said, and he and the holy man, both laid down on their bed rolls.

My body was tired from traveling, and my head was tired from thinking of this village. I lay down on my bedroll, and closed my eyes. I heard the holy man breathing, and knew he slept. The cool air blew across my face and felt good, I turned on my side, and soon fell into darkness.

We stood on the sand, watching the boats slide out into the water. The villagers had loaded the boats in darkness, and now left under the sun's new light . The water was calm, with only small waves rolling in. The elders said this was a good sign. Kekoa told the elders he would return, after they had built the new village.

"Build strong boats." he told them, "you will travel back with us."

The grandmothers stood together, with water rolling down their faces, waving and calling out to their children. The grandfathers helped push the boats into the water, and now stood watching as they went into the sea. My heart hurt watching this, and my eyes filled with water. I took in a deep breath and blew it out, then looked at Konani.

He was returning to the old man, who sat outside his hut, slowly shaking his head from side to side, I followed Konani, and joined him with the old man.

"I am ready," he said, "to pass."

Konani nodded, yet did not speak.

"The young have left," he looked at me, "I will not see them run and laugh."

"You will build boats, fish, and keep the village until they return." Konani told him.

The old man looked out to the water, "I will not see them return."

"You will watch them with the ancestors." Konani said.

The old man smiled, "Yes! I will do this!"

Konani clapped him on the back, "We go."

"Travel well." the old man said.

We went into the new mother's hut. She smiled, yet her eyes were full of water. A young man stood by her, and the baby.

"Are you stronger?" Konani asked.

"I am stronger," she said, "yet not strong to travel in the boats."

The young man looked at us, "I will take them to the sea caves."

"Can you walk?" Konani asked.

The young man spoke, "I will pull them on branches strapped together." he said.

"I have seen this." Konani said, "When you reach the sea caves, give her fish each day and help her walk to get stronger."

Konani dug in his basket, and gave the young man a pouch of the ground leaves, and many fresh leaves.

"Make tea for her to drink when she eats."

The young man nodded.

"Learn the leaves, and gather more." Konani told him.

We left, and walked to the hut, were the hot baby was. The mother and baby were not in the hut. Then we went to the hut where Konani gave medicine for an old woman's sore bones, and she was not there.

"She is with the others." Konani said, and looked toward the water.

Many grandmothers sat on logs, around the fire pit, drinking tea and talking. He pointed to her, and we walked to the women. Konani looked at them

"Where is the baby that was hot?" he asked.

"The medicine cooled her," a grandmother said, "my daughter left in the boat with her."

"Do you need medicine?" He asked.

"Our hearts hurt," a woman said, then the others joined her, "Yes, our hearts hurt!"

"I have no medicine for this." he told them.

We heard the holy man, and looked to see him, walking with the grandfathers from the water. They joined us at the fire pit. The holy man stood next to the fire, and raised his arms up.

"Ancestors!" he yelled, "Come to us!"

I was surprised, I had not heard him yell with such power.

"Protect this village. Guide and protect the young that have left."

He stopped and looked at them, "Make them strong, and let them see their families return." then dropped his arms.

The grandfathers and grandmothers cried out, "Let us see our children!"

The holy man raised his arms again, and the villagers were quiet. He closed his eyes, and did not speak. We did not move, we watched the holy man, and waited. Then he took much air into his chest, and pushed it out quickly with his mouth.

"The ancestors are with your young, I have seen the island where they go." he spoke quickly, "it has fish and fruit, and clear water from the mountain."

He opened his eyes, "They will be safe."

The grandmothers and grandfathers cried out, and were happy, then the holy man spoke again.

"There will be warriors that come. They will wear feathers on their heads."

The grandfathers began to shake their heads, and look at each other, with anger in their eyes.

"You will welcome them as travelers, you will give them food, and let them sit at your fire pit."

An old man shouted, "They made our young leave!"

"Your young will return, to take you to the new village."

The man looked at him, "You have seen this?"

"Yes, not all will travel, yet many will."

The villagers nodded, and listened carefully.

"You will not say the name Kekoa!" the holy man shouted again, "Tell the chief's son that the young passed with sickness."

"We will say that." an old man said, and looked at the others nodding their heads.

"I will warn other villages of the young war birds that come," the holy man said, "then I will return."

The holy man looked at Konani and I.

"Get our baskets and bedrolls."

Konani and I left the fire pit, and I heard the holy man tell them.

"The ancestors will protect you."

# CHAPTER 6

We left, and walked toward my home village. The trail climbed up, and wound around the base of the mountain, and I looked back. I saw the grandfathers and grandmothers still sitting at the fire pit, and I wondered what would happen when the chief's son arrived. The holy man told them he would come soon, looking for Kekoa.

"Then he will follow us to your village." he told me.

We must travel fast, and our baskets were heavy with medicine.

"Can he catch us?" I wondered.

I wanted to warn my family, and I wanted the holy man to help the villagers prepare. I thought of my mother, and wanted to feel her arms around me. I wanted to look into her face, see her smile, and make me feel safe.

"Ancestors," I thought, "protect my family."


I WAS glad we traveled fast, yet I felt hot, and my back was wet. The blanket slipped down, and the basket rubbed on my skin again, so I reached back, grabbed the blanket, and pulled it up.

"I will not stop." I told myself.

I walked fast, to stay behind the holy man and Konani. The basket swung with my steps, so I grabbed it to hold, while I walked. They carried baskets heavier than mine, yet they had longer legs, and could travel fast.

After my ceremony, I knew they were my brothers, in the circle of medicine men. I was blessed to have the holy man and Konani as my teachers, and I wanted to show them I was not a weak boy.

"Will mother see me as a boy?" I wondered.

Many big moons had passed since I left her, and I was stronger now. I wanted her to see me as a medicine man, and be happy that I had learned of the ancestors, and my teacher.

"I will tell her what I learned." I thought, "she will sit by me, and give me fruit and fish."

This made me smile, and I wanted to fly as the sea birds to my village.

WE REACHED TREES, and walked under them, on dirt wet with a small stream of water. The holy man dropped his basket, and followed the water up, to where it bubbled out of the rocks. Konani and I followed, and we soon splashed cold water on our faces .

"Aww," Konani said as he cooled himself down, then splashed a little water at me.

I laughed, and enjoyed the feeling of it.

The holy man stretched his arms up and around, then bent from the waist over to touch the ground with his fingers. He hung like this, looking at the dirt, then slowly rose to stand.

"Do this." he told us, and put his arms up again.

Konani and I raised our arms up, then bent over to touch our hands to the ground. This pulled on my back, and felt good. We hung over like this, then Konani looked at me and laughed,

"We look like birds pecking at the ground!"

The holy man reached into his bag, and pulled some leaves out. He handed Konani and I a leaf.

"Chew this, then spit it out" he said, "It will help us walk."

71

I looked at my leaf, and knew it from the medicine man camp.

"You make tea with this." I put it in my mouth, bit down, it did not taste good.

The holy man lifted his basket, and looked at my face.

"Watch Konani, when he spits it out, you can also." he told me.

Konani and I put our baskets on, and followed the medicine man. I felt good after the water, and pulling on my back. I chewed the tea leaf as I walked, and it mixed with the water in my mouth. We traveled fast, not speaking, and watched where we put our feet on the trail.

Konani turned his head, spit the leaves off the side of the trail, and kept walking. I spit my leaves out also.

"The birds will eat them now!" I said.

"Kekoa taught me to speak like a bird," Konani said, "I will teach you."

"Good."

"Listen to the birds, then call out their songs."

I listened to the birds flying around us, then sang as they did.

Konani laughed hard, "Your bird sounds sick!"

I laughed hard also, and heard the holy man laughing.

"Kai," the holy man yelled back, "your bird needs medicine!"


THE TRAIL LED us along the top of the high mountain. I looked down, and saw the sun low to the water.

"We will stop soon." the holy man said.

"We will fill our water pouches," Konani said, "and eat fruit from the trees."

I thought of the place we slept, when they led me from my village, and my family.

"I will sleep good." I told them.

My shoulders hurt from the weight of the basket, and my legs were tired, yet I had walked the hard part of the trail. After the sun rises again, we will walk down the mountain to my village.

"Your mother will be happy to see your face!" Konani said.

"I will be happy to see her!"

I thought of the holy man warning my village, and I wondered what they would do. Kekoa had left. Who would guide them to a new island? They were not prepared to fight, and I feared for their safety.

"I am glad the holy man is guided by the ancestors," I thought, "he will speak their words so we can hear."

The ancestors whisper in our thoughts to guide us, yet when the holy man speaks, their words are clear.

"I want to hear their whispers clearly." I thought.

WE HAD STOPPED to sleep when the last light from the sun went away, and woke before it returned. We had traveled far and fast, and I looked ahead, to see where we walked. I knew when the trail turned around the bottom of the mountain, I would be above the village. The village of my family.

"I am not the boy that left," I thought, "will they still see me as a boy?"

The villagers did not know we were coming, and we came to warn them, yet I was happy to be back. I heard voices from the trail ahead, and listened as I walked. Just ahead the trailed turned, and I wanted to see who traveled. The holy man stopped, and he spoke. I tried to look past Konani, but could not see who spoke to the holy man. Then Konani stepped closer to the holy man, and I saw a friend.

"Aikane!" I shouted and smiled.

He and another boy from the village, stood on the trail, and my friend's eyes grew big when he saw me.

"Kai" he yelled.

The boys turned, and ran back down the trail to the village.

"They will know we come." I said, as we walked around the turn, and I saw my village.

The long leaves on trees blew with the wind from the water. I saw huts under the trees, and heard children playing. I smelled the fire pit, fish cooking, and saw boats pulled up on the sand. The water was the color of the sky, and I wanted to swim in it.

The trail reached the bottom of the mountain, and we walked on

73

flat dirt. We passed the trail that led to the waterfall, and as we walked by, I thought of when I ran there to sit by the water. My heart pounded in my chest, and I wanted to see my family.

We walked by huts, and I knew we would come to my mother's hut soon. Then I saw my father, and older brothers. They walked quickly to us. I smiled, yet they did not smile back. They walked fast and reached the holy man ahead of me.

"My woman is sick" father told him.

My head jerked back, "Mother?" Sick?

"Take me to her." the holy man said.

Father turned to walk ahead of the holy man, and my brothers waited for Konani to pass, then came to me.

"You are big!" my brother said.

I nodded, "Mother is sick?"

"She cannot rise from her mat," my other brother told me.

"She has not spoken, and cannot get up."

"No!" I cried out, and pushed past them.

They followed me, as I walked fast down the trail.

I spoke to my teacher silently, "Can we help her?"

"She will go with her sister." my teacher told me.

I caught up to Konani, and walked behind him. My heart hurt, and my eyes filled with water. My mother's sister had been sick such as this. Her lip hung down on her face, and she did not speak. My mother had pulled her sister to sit up, yet her arm and leg hung down from her body. She passed to live with the ancestors after this, and my mother worked hard to care for her sister's children, along with her own.

"The medicine will help." I thought, "we have much medicine to give her."

We were close to my father's hut.

"I will make her tea, and talk to her." I told myself.


FATHER and the holy man went into the hut. I walked with Konani, and dropped my basket by the doorway. Konani stood back so I could walk in. Father and the holy man stood next to her mat with their backs to me, I walked behind them, looking to see my mother's face. She saw me, and I bit my lip. I closed my eyes to keep the water from falling, then looked back at her. Her eyes also had water, and she tried to speak, yet no words came from her. I grabbed her hand, her eyes watched me, yet her face and body did not move.

"Make tea." the holy man told Konani.

I heard Konani walk out, and saw the holy man go around to stand on the other side of mother. He held his hands in the air over her face, then slowly moved his hands through the air over her body to her feet. My mother watched the holy man, and he smiled at her.

"The ancestors make a home for you" he told her.

Her eyes looked from him, to my father.

"She is yet young," my father said and touched her hair, "she cannot go."

My chest was heavy, and I tried to take breath in, yet it was hard.

The holy man looked at him. "Her sister waits."

"Her sister?" my father said, and shook his head.

"Her sister will guide her" the holy man told him.

Maka cried out, "No! She cannot go!"

I looked at her standing by the door, and saw other sisters, brothers and children my mother had raised up behind her. Water fell from my eyes, and I fell down to my knees, laying my head on her hand.

"No, no!" my brother called out, and the others also cried out loud.

The holy man threw his arms up, and yelled, "Quiet!"

They stopped, and the holy man spoke to them. "Her body will pass soon, she will go to live with her sister."

The holy man looked at my mother, nodded at her, then back at us, "She will watch over you." he told us.

I looked at her, and her face was at peace. The holy man stepped to the door, "Come to see her, yet be at peace, so she will be ready to pass."

. . .

THE HOLY MAN walked to my father, and waved for them to come by mother. They stood around her, and I sat beside her, holding her hand.

The holy man put his hand on mother's eyes, "Close your eyes, and see your sister"

The holy man held his hand over her eyes. "She waits for you."

He took his hand away, and her eyes were closed. I saw her chest move with air, and was glad she had not left. I looked at her face, and my heart wanted to go with her. My shoulders began to shake, I heard a noise, yet did not know it came from my own mouth. Konani brought in the pot with tea. The holy man put a hand up to Konani, he turned, and put the pot in the corner.

Mother's eyes were closed, and she looked asleep. Sitting on the floor close to her, I watched her chest rise with each breath, and I looked at her face. I saw her eyes, nose and mouth, thinking of when she laughed and smiled. I looked at her arms, thought how she wrapped them around me, and I felt safe.

"You were a good mother" I told her.

Father, her children, and I stayed by her, knowing she would leave us soon. We watched her last breaths, while the sun's light slowly left the hut.


MOTHER WAS GONE. Konani stood by me, and the holy man stood near mother, and her children. My brother had run out of the hut wailing, and down to the water, where he still sat on the sand. My father sat on the floor next to mother, while villagers came into the hut to see her. I put my lips on her hand, then stood, and walked out of the hut into the night.

I walked to a tree, and slid down to sit. I did not want her to go, yet when she left us, I wondered what her travels would be like. The holy man said her sister would guide her, he told us the ancestors had prepared a home for her. I knew only her body had passed, and that she still lived, yet I wanted her with me now.

"If I had not left," I thought, and water came into my eyes, "I would have been with her longer."

My teacher softly brushed my shoulder.

"The ancestors called for you to leave," she said, "they called for her also."

Water rolled down my face, and I wiped it away.

"Mother," I called out to her, "I will see you when I pass."

I closed my eyes, leaned against the tree, and I thought of how I came to be here. The ancestors knew I would learn to care for myself, learn medicine, have the holy man and Konani as new brothers, and meet Kekoa .

"I am blessed to learn this before she passed." I told them, "thank you."

I heard foot steps in the dark, and looked to see the holy man.

"Kai" he said, "sit with your father and family."

I stood up, and the holy man put his hand on my shoulder, "You will help them."

I nodded, and walked into the hut.


FATHER SAT NEXT TO MOTHER, leaning over to rest his head on his arms. Many others also sat near her, and much water fell from their eyes. I walked to them, and my father looked at me.

"I will not see her again." he said softly.

I put my hand on his shoulder. He looked into my eyes, shaking his head. I felt my teacher, and heard her say, "She waits at the tree."

I looked at my father, yet I did not know what to say.

"She waits at the tree." my teacher said again.

I took in a breath, and blew the air out, and spoke, "She waits at the tree."

He looked at me, "The tree?"

"The tree." I said again, not knowing of what I spoke.

My father's eyes opened wide, he looked at her, then back at me.

"I will go." he said, and stood up.

Jatu watched father leave. "Where does he go?"

"He will return."

I looked at mother, saw she was not there, and knew she left with her sister. The torch outside sent streaks of light in through the door, and I felt I was in a dream. I heard sounds from my family, and felt their sad hearts. I looked around at them, and wanted them to know they would see her again.

"Why do the ancestors not live with us?" I thought, then I heard my teacher.

"We are not gone," she said, "we are here"

MY BODY WAS tired from traveling, my heart was tired from watching my mother pass, and I could not eat the fish given to me. My brother returned from sitting by the water, lay down on his mat in the hut, and others put mats down to sleep next to mother on the floor. I sat in the darkness, and waited for father to return. I listened to them breathing, looked around the hut, and thought of growing here as a child. Mother prepared the fish and fruit here, she watched over me, and she filled the hut with the good feelings that Konani spoke of. Mother stayed near the hut, teaching the girls. Father and my brothers left the hut when they awoke, and went to fish or sit by the fire pit. I wondered what my father and family would do now.

Konani walked in the doorway of the hut, "Kai" he whispered, "we sleep now."

"I will join you after father returns."

Konani nodded and left.

I closed my eyes, and breathed quietly. Then in my head, I saw myself standing on sand. I watched long boats travel across the water to me, and I looked around. I stood with villagers, waiting for the boats. They were the grandfathers and grandmothers that had stayed, when their young left the island. I looked back to the water, and saw the boats close now. A young woman, with long black hair, sat in a boat with the men. I saw her strong arms holding a paddle, digging it into the water, and pushing it back. Her paddle moved smoothly, like the men that sat around her. I looked hard to see her face.

"Kai" my father whispered, as he shook my shoulder.

My eyes opened, I had not heard him enter the hut. Father waved for me to come out of the hut. I followed him, and he turned to wrap his arms around me.

"I saw her." he said, and let go.

I looked at his face, and he was smiling.

"She was under the tree," he told me, "she will wait for me in the ancestors' village."

"She said this?"

"Yes," he nodded, "after she left, I sat down and did not leave."

I nodded, "You wanted her to come back."

"Will you stay with us?" he asked.

"No, the holy man and Konani, still teach me."

Father nodded, "I am glad you will be a medicine man."

I smiled, he did not know that I was.

Father put his hand on my shoulder, "Sleep." he said, and walked into the hut.

I watched him go inside, and was glad that he saw mother.

"He will have peace."

I thought of her, living with the ancestors, waiting for father to join her.

"Will I see you?" I asked, "will you come to me?"

I walked from the hut, down the trail, to where the holy man and Konani slept. I heard the waves, and looked at the light, coming down from the moon on the water.

Then I looked up at the night sky, with the bright lights that sparkled.

"Are you there?" I wondered.


THE SUN ROSE, and did not know that our mother left us. The sea did not know my mother no longer watched her man push his boat out to fish, and the trees did not know she would not walk under them to pick fruit. The birds sang their songs, and the children ran playing on the sand. When a traveler came to our village, he would not know that a woman who made many hearts happy, was not there. I felt a hole in my chest that mother filled, and I thought of her soft arms. I knew my family felt this also.

Women brought food to us. We finished eating, and Konani walked with me, back to my family hut. Many women prepared my mother's body. She would be carried to the cave, where our ancestors had been placed. After that we would have a feast, and large fire in the fire pit. The fire would burn into the night, so she could see us from the other side, and know we honored her.

My head and heart did not know how to think or feel. I felt my body, yet I was not in it. "Am I dreaming?" I wondered.

I walked with my father, family and villagers through the trees, watched them place her wrapped body in the cave, and seal it with large rocks. Women and children threw flowers on the rocks, many touching the rocks, and speaking to mother before they left. We returned to the village, where I sat at the fire pit, and listened to men and women speak of mother.

Many stories of her were told, of when she was young, and before she was a mother. I had not heard of her in this way, and now saw my mother as a young woman, as well as my mother. She had a good life, a happy life, in this village. She joined with my father, she brought children in, and cared for them well. She smiled much, and villagers said that she would now live in their hearts. Hot fish was served by women in the village, and my sisters made fruit and cold fish, the way mother taught them.

"Good!" The villagers said, licking their fingers, and smacking their lips loudly.

This would let mother know she taught her children well. We ate, and a strong fruit juice was passed around to drink. My brother handed the juice to me, I took a sip and my mouth burned. I felt the juice travel down into my belly. I handed the drink back to my brother, who drank it again, then gave it to the man next to him.

Konani did not leave me. He did not speak, yet he made me feel good. Konani knew when to speak, and when to be quiet. He had a healing of his own, that was not the medicine of plants. He gave this healing through comfort, as my mother had. I wanted to learn this from him.

"Thank you" I told Konani.

Konani smiled, and put his hand on my shoulder. "My mother also lives with the ancestors."

I nodded, and knew he had felt as I did

THE HOLY MAN STOOD, and raised his hands.

"I will speak of village safety." he said, dropping his hands, the villagers stopped talking and looked at him.

"We came to warn you of a war bird that comes." he yelled out.

I watched the faces of the men, and knew they were not prepared.

"Who is this war bird?" an elder asked.

"The son of a chief that has passed." the holy man said, and looked around.

"He comes for battle?" a man asked.

"He would be chief of all villages on this island."

The villagers shouted out, "No!" "We will not have a chief!"

"He has many warriors, and they will fight for your village and women."

The men jumped to their feet, "We will fight!" they called out.

The holy man raised his arms again, "Sit!"

A man still stood, and looked at the holy man, "If they travel the high trail, they will not come here."

The holy man nodded, "You must be prepared."

"I will send my grandsons to watch the high and low trails." an elder said.

"This is good," the holy man said, and he told the villagers of Kekoa taking the young from the other village, on the sea to another island."

"We cannot do this." an elder said.

"The elders will tell the chief's son a great sickness took their young," the holy man said, and looked around, "you must hide your young, and say the sickness made your young pass."

The men were quiet, looking at each other, nodding.

"We will hide our young when he comes." an elder spoke loudly, so all would hear him.

"Yes!" shouted another.

"Good," the holy man said, "Do not fight, and do not say the name Kekoa."

"The women will prepare to leave for the mountain caves."

I looked at my sisters, and saw fear on their faces.

"When they come, travel fast," the holy man told them, "Grandmothers and grandfathers will stay in the village."

They nodded, "We will tell them our young passed from the sickness."

THERE WAS no moon this night, and darkness came down on us. The flames grew bigger, the wood popped loudly, and we moved back from the heat. My father and brothers, threw more branches and dry wood on the fire, until the flames reached higher than my father's head.

"She will see that" my father yelled, and he and my brothers, were happy with the large fire.

My father came to me, handing me a large branch to put on the fire.

"Let her see this!" he said.

I turned and threw the wood into the fire, watching it start to burn. The flames were bright in the dark night, my eyes followed them up to where the smoke left, and was blown away with the wind.

"She sees us." I told him.

My father put his arm around my shoulder, and said, "I feel her."

I looked up at him, saw a small smile on his lips, yet his eyes were sad.

WHEN I LAY down to sleep, I thought, "Standing by the fire with my father, is the vision I will hold."

I saw it again in my mind. I did not know if he would pass after I left the village, I did not know if he would be safe when the chief's son came. I turned on my side, then the other side, yet thoughts came into my head and chased sleep away. I took in a big breath, and turned to lay on my back. Lights in the sky looked down at me.

"Mother," I whispered, "I know you will protect them."

My heart suddenly warmed, water came into my eyes, and I knew she was with me.

I swallowed, and felt her next to me.

"Thank you," I whispered, and water rolled out of my eyes, "thank you."

WE WERE READY TO LEAVE. Maka handed me fresh fruit, and wrapped her arms around me. I felt her, and thought of mother. Brothers, sisters and others, stood around and told me, "Travel well."

Then father came to me, and clapped me on the arm. "She watches over you."

I smiled at him, "I know."

He had water in his eyes, yet he smiled, "Travel well."

The holy man called out to them, "Be safe." and turned to walk on the trail.

"Thank you!" Konani said, smiling and waving at the villagers as he walked away.

I looked at father and my family, and nodded, "I will return."

I turned to walk away and felt them still watching me. My heart hurt from leaving them, and it also hurt from knowing that when I returned, mother would not be there. I did not look back at them, or the village. I was ready to leave, and let my heart heal. Yet, as I walked, water fell from my eyes.

"You will see new villages." Konani called back to me.

I knew he wanted to help me think of this, and not my mother.

"Good." I called back, wiped my eyes, and thought, "She is with me."

# CHAPTER 7

We traveled quickly beside the water, then turned to follow the trail into the mountain. As we walked up, the air got warmer, and heavy with water. My face felt wet from it, and I looked around at the plants, whose leaves had water drops on them. Plants covered the ground, and many plants grew up the trees. Tall trees stood with plants that grew on them, hanging their leaves from the branches. I breathed in, smelled flowers, and looked to see them growing among the many plants. I looked ahead, and saw that we walked toward clouds that hung low on the trail.

"We will pick these." The holy man said, and pointed to a low growing plant, with small leaves and flowers.

I was happy to drop my basket, and begin to pick the leaves.

"Pick the flowers also." the holy man said.

Konani and I filled a basket, then the holy man took it from us. He reached into the basket, grabbed them, and squeezed. He did this with all leaves and flowers until they were small balls, then he dropped them into a pouch in his large basket. The holy man swung his basket on to his back, and starting walking.

I drank water, and soon followed Konani. The trail was not wide, tree roots grew over it, and I had to watch where I put my feet. I heard sounds of water, and looked to see a stream, yet it was hidden by bushes. As we walked into the mountain, the trail got smaller. The plants and trees grew close to it, and the air did not move. Water dripped from my face, and I wiped it with my hand. The blanket on my back was wet under the basket, and my arms and legs also felt wet. I grabbed my water pouch, drank again, yet it did not cool me. The holy man stopped, and pointed to small fruit hanging on trees, and many laying on the ground under it.

"Pick the soft ones, and drink the juice." he told us.

I dropped my basket, and the blanket stuck to my back. Konani saw this, and pulled at it. The holy man had picked a fruit, sucked the juice from it, and smiled. I saw juice running down his hand. I picked one, bit into it, and sweet juice filled my mouth.

"Good!" I quickly drank all the juice I could squeeze from it.

I picked another, then another. The juice ran down my face, and covered my hands .

"When your body pours out water, it is good to drink the juice of fruit." the holy man told us.

"Fruit is good medicine also." he said.

"Fruit?" I asked.

"Fruit that is soft and sweet."

Konani held his fruit out, and squeezed so the juice ran out, "Hold it over their mouth, and give it to sick villagers."

"And babies." the holy man said.

"Are you as tired now?" Konani asked me.

"No."

"The Great Mother gave us this fruit," the holy man said, "she cares for us."

I thought of my mother, and how she gave me fruit, "Does Great Mother live with the ancestors?" I asked.

"Great Mother grows the trees that give us fruit, she grows the fish for us to eat," he said.

"The water to drink." Konani said.

"She lives with the ancestors?"

The holy man shook his head, "She is the dirt, she is the water."

"Oh," I knew this, "Father is the sky, the sun, and the moon."

The holy man smiled, "Yes."


KONANI PUT the blanket on my back, then the basket. The blanket was still wet, yet the basket did not feel as heavy. We walked quicker now, the holy man held his basket with both hands, and leaned forward as he walked. I took more steps, to keep up with their long legs. My breath came in and out stronger, yet I stayed behind Konani, and was happy with myself. I listened to the birds, and to the holy man, speak of plants that we passed.

"Tea." he said, and pointed to a bush, then, "Put on cuts." he pointed to another.


MOTHER CAME into my thoughts much. When I thought of her, water came into my eyes, and my heart hurt. I left her to learn from the holy man, and thought she would be there when I returned. I thought how she put fish and fruit in my basket for my travel. I wanted to see her smile, sit with her, and tell her of what I had learned.

"She would be happy that I am a medicine man." I told myself.

"She knows this." my teacher whispered.

"Yes," I nodded, "she sees me."

The sun went behind the mountain, and the light was going away. The holy man saw a place under the trees that did not have bushes, and went to it.

"We make camp." he said.

"Fill the water pouches." he told us, and handed Konani his.

Konani and I dropped our baskets by the holy man, and walked toward the sound of the water. We found a small, clear stream running over rocks, and filled the pouches. Konani put them down, washed his face and arms, and I did also. The water felt good, and I wanted to wash my body, yet darkness was falling so I followed Konani back to the holy man.

When we returned, the holy man was burning bound dried leaves, that he held in his hand. He waved the smoke with the feather, and asked the ancestors to be with us, and protect us. I had not seen him do this when we traveled before.

"Why does he do this?" I asked Konani.

"So we sleep well." Konani said, yet said no more.

I gathered wood for a small fire, which Konani started. Konani poked at the burning wood until there was a good pile to set the tea pot on. The holy man gathered leaves from plants and bushes, then washed them in the stream of water.

"Eat these with the dried fish." he said, and smiled.

He handed me many wet leaves, then Konani. I watched him take a bite of dried fish, then put the leaves in his mouth and chew. I grabbed my dried fish from the basket, took a bite, followed by a bite of the leaves. I tasted the sea on my fish, mixed with the fresh leaves. I was happy with this food, and the leaves helped fill my belly. Konani poured tea into our large half shells, I held the edge of mine, and sipped the hot tea. I liked to travel with the holy man and Konani. I liked traveling to see new parts of the island, and eating new food.

We sat in darkness around the small fire. I watched the fire, listened to Konani and the holy man speak of the mountain village, then Konani turned to me.

"We will arrive when the sun is high."

The holy man rubbed his eyes, and lay down on his bed roll.

"Sleep." Konani told me, and laid down.

"I will sleep good" I told them, and they laughed.

I lay down, closed my eyes, and felt sleep coming. I heard whispers! I quickly opened my eyes, and looked across the fire, to see Konani looking back at me. He nodded his head, and put his finger to his mouth. I looked at the holy man, and he lay on his side, with his back to us.

Again, the I heard the whispers.

"Villagers?" I asked, and looked at Konani.

He shook his head, and whispered, "No."

I thought of the chief's son, and my eyes opened wide, "The chief's son?"

The holy man rolled over, and looked at me. "The ancestors of the village we travel to, do not sleep."

My mouth fell open.

"They will not hurt us." Konani said.

I looked around, and was glad that I traveled with the holy man and Konani, who knew of this.

The holy man closed his eyes. Konani smiled at me, pulled his blanket up around his neck, before closing his eyes. I looked carefully into the darkness, and did not see the ancestors. I listened to their whispers, they were not happy, I felt their hearts hurt.

"Ancestors not happy?" I thought, "why are they not happy?" I pulled the blanket up, closed my eyes, and soon slept.

I AWOKE TO LOUD BIRDS, sun streaming in through the trees, and hot air. My face was wet, and stuck to my arm. I moved my arm, wiped my face with my hands, and sat up.

Konani was putting broken branches on the fire, and waving his hand over them to start burning. The holy man was not here, and I saw his bed roll was ready to travel.

"Did you sleep?" Konani asked.

"Yes." I said, and rolled up my blanket.

"I dreamed of the ancestors here," Konani said, " I dreamed there was a great sickness, and many villagers passed."

"I felt their hearts hurt." I told him.

Konani put the tea pot on the hot wood, and I put my bed roll next to my basket, as the holy man walked to us. He handed us the sweet fruit that we drank juice from.

"Many fruits grow on the mountain," he said, and took a bite, "this is the sweetest."

I enjoyed the sweet juice, then the holy man handed us nuts from his basket, and we sipped the tea that Konani made.

"We go to the mountain village," the holy man said, "I will speak to them of the chief's son, then we will leave."

"We will not eat or sleep there?" I asked.

The holy man shook his head, "Sickness is in the village."

Konani watched me, "We will give them medicine."

"Yes" the holy man said, "then leave."

We finished our tea, and Konani kicked dirt on the fire. The holy man started down the trail, and Konani looked at me.

"Ready?"

I nodded my head, and walked behind him. I wanted to see this village, and know of the sickness the holy man spoke of. I wanted to know why the ancestors could not sleep, and whispered of their hearts hurting.

I HEARD sounds of children playing as we came closer to the village. The path was bigger now, and I saw many marks from the villagers that walked on it. The trail opened, and I saw the children, women and men, as we walked into a clearing. The clearing was in the center of the village, with a large fire pit. There were big and small huts, built around it. The women stopped working to look at us, and children ran to us, a little boy came to me with a big smile, and I saw wounds on his nose and ears.

"Welcome," an old man said.

The holy man put his hand on the old man's shoulder, "Thank you."

The villagers covered their bodies with cloth here, I saw men and women with cloth hanging from their necks. I looked at the old man speaking, then down to a large wound on his leg, with thick water in it.

I looked up at Konani, and he whispered to me, "The sickness."

I nodded, and looked around. Not all the villagers had this sickness, yet many did. Some villagers had only small wounds, yet others had arms or legs that were eaten by this sickness. A woman sat outside her hut, with hands that pulled into her body. Others had fingers or toes that were gone, and I saw dark fingers on a little boy.

The holy man looked at us, "Give medicine." then he looked back at the old man, and began to speak of the chief's son.

89

Konani nodded, grabbed my arm, and looked down at me, "Do not take water or food from the villagers."

I thought of the sickness that many of my ancestors passed with.

"Is this the sickness that took my ancestors?"

"No," Konani said, "your ancestors had a sickness that passed with them, this sickness does not leave. Their ancestors had it, the grand-parents have it, and the young."

We walked to an old woman sitting outside her hut.

"Do your hands hurt?" Konani asked.

"My hands, my feet, and body hurts."

Konani put down his basket, and reached into it, grabbing a pouch with leaves. He gave her the pouch. "Make tea with these. After you drink, take the hot leaves from the pot, and put them on your sore bones."

She nodded and smiled, many of her teeth were gone, and her lips were thick.

"Thank you."

"Is there a villager that cannot come out of their hut?" Konani asked.

The woman pointed to a small hut, "A girl."

We walked across the center of the village, and I saw the holy man sitting at the fire pit with many men.

Konani asked a woman outside the hut, "A girl is sick?"

She took us in the hut, and as I walked in, a bad smell came to me. I saw a small body, under a blanket, laying on a mat. She was on her side with her back to us, and the bad smell came from her.

"You are her mother?" Konani asked.

The woman nodded her head, and leaned down to shake the girl's shoulder. The girl made a noise, then her mother started to turn her.

"Oh!" the girl cried out. The girl bent her legs, and lay back.

"Oh!" I said, and covered my mouth with my hand.

The sickness had eaten this little girl's face. She had no nose, and a large wound covered her lips and mouth. Her eyes sank down, and did not shine.

"Can she eat?" Konani asked.

"I chew for her," the mother said, "like a baby."

"Bring water and wash her body," Konani said, "wash her blanket."

The mother nodded.

Konani looked inside his basket, and pulled out the sweet fruit we drank juice from.

He sat down next to the girl, "Drink." he said, and squeezed the juice into her mouth.

"Give her juice from fruit, and water," Konani told her mother, "Wash her, and take her outside in the sun."

Konani looked hard at the girl's mother, "Care for her."

Then he grabbed his basket, and we walked from the hut, "The mother waits for the girl to pass." he said, and shook his head, "she will not care for her."

"She will not care for her?"

"No, " Konani said, "I spoke for the girl, yet her mother will not listen."

He kicked the dirt, and shook his head. I looked at him, and had not seen his face like this. He looked like he wanted to fight, kicked the dirt again, and pulled his hands into fists.

"This mother is bad!" he told me, and walked quickly away.

"Bad!" I said, and ran to walk with him.


My mother had cared for me. When I was sick, she gave me fruit, and rubbed my back. I thought of the little girl, with a great sickness, and yet her mother does not care for her. He spoke no more of the girl, yet I know his heart hurt for her. We saw women, and asked of the sick in the village. We saw many villagers, giving them medicines for their wounds, and to make tea. Konani gave all his medicine to the villagers, then we started to give the medicines that I carried. We walked out of a hut, and saw the holy man waited for us.

"We go." he told us.

"I am glad to leave." Konani said.

"We have given Konanis medicine, and now give what is in my basket." I told the holy man.

"I have warned of the chief's son," the holy man spoke to us, and many villagers started gathered around.

The holy man smiled and raised his hands, "The ancestors will protect you, and I ask they send away your sickness."

The villagers were happy to hear this, and followed us, as we walked slowly from the village. They did not want us to leave, and asked us to eat a feast with them.

"We must travel," the holy man said, "and warn another village of the chief's son."

The villagers waved, and yelled, "Travel well."


WE WALKED FROM THE VILLAGE, I looked back, and saw the villagers still watched us. I was glad to travel again, and wanted to see a new village, and the other side of the island. We walked through trees, and the trail came to a cleared area next to a stream. Women squatted next to the water, washing clothes, and filling pots of water. Children played in the water, splashing themselves and laughing.

"Should I fill our water pouches?" I asked.

"The water has sickness." the holy man said, and we kept walking.

"I will carry your basket." Konani told me, and took his off. He handed me his basket, and I gave him mine. His basket carried no medicine, and it felt good on my back. We walked down the trail, and Konani told the holy man of the little girl.

"Her mother does not care for her," Konani called out, "she waits for her to pass!"

The holy man nodded, "The mother's heart has much pain."

"The girl has pain!" Konani said, "Why does the mother not care for her?"

The holy man stopped, and turned to Konani, "The mother cannot see her child like this, and she stays away."

Konani shook his head, "I do not..."

The holy man put his hand on Konani's shoulder, "The mother's heart cannot hold the pain of another child passing," he looked at me, "she cannot."

"The girl?" Konani asked.

"She will pass soon," the holy man said, "and feel no more pain, yet her mother's pain will stay."

"I did not think of the mother's pain." Konani said.

The holy man smiled, turned, and walked on.

Konani looked at me, "I have much to learn."

We came to fruit trees, and the holy man picked many, throwing them into my basket.

"Eat." he said, and handed me a piece of fruit.

I had not seen this fruit, and bit into it. "Good!"

Konani and the holy man also ate, and I reached for another.

"Do not eat more," the holy man said, "your body does not know this fruit."

"You put the fruit in here" Konani pointed to his mouth, "and it comes out here." he pointed around to his bottom, and laughed.

After we finished, we walked until we saw a small waterfall.

"Fill the water pouches." the holy man told me.

We put down our baskets, and walked to the small pool of water, at the bottom of the waterfall. The holy man walked into the water, and sat down in it, leaning his head back until it covered his face. Konani and I waited for the holy man to wash, then we did the same. The water was cool, and felt good on my body. I washed away the dirt, and smell of sickness. I was glad that I did not live in that village, and now I knew why the ancestors there were not happy. We ate dried fish, and picked more fruit for my basket.


As we walked, I thought of what I had seen, and how Konani spoke to the villagers.

"He is a good teacher." I thought.

The holy man has taught me much, and now I learned from Konani. I felt glad the ancestors picked me to learn medicine. I have traveled to new villages, and the holy man and Konani have been good teachers.

"Thank you." I whispered.

The trail led us down the mountain, and I was glad to be away from the mountain village. The air got cooler, with wind that blew up from the sea, and every step took me closer to a new village.

"There." the holy man pointed, "we will gather medicine."

I looked down the mountain to where he pointed, and saw a clearing in the trees. We walked on, and I smelled the sea. I could not see it, yet felt glad to return to the water. The trail took a turn, and we walked to the clearing, that I had seen from above. The holy man led us from the dirt of the trail to mud, where he walked toward tall grasses, and reeds. He stopped, and turned to us.

"Gather the mud under the warm water."

"Eggs?" Konani asked.

"Yes," the holy man said, "Kai will help me."

We dropped the baskets from our backs to the ground, and the holy man reached inside for a small basket to carry.

"Bring another basket." he said to me, so I grabbed an empty basket to carry.

The holy man took off his sandals, and I did also. He led me into the tall grass, the mud squeezed up between my toes. I watched where the holy man put his feet in the mud, and the mark would fill with water before I put my foot down. The mud was getting warmer, and had a new color, that made me think of the sky just before the sun goes down. The holy man stopped, and I stepped beside him to look at the pool of water. It was hot, and the water bubbled up across the pool. He squatted down at the edge of the water, and scooped up mud in his hand.

"Squeeze the water from it." he told me.

I watched him squeeze the water from the mud, and it became a ball in his hand. He put the ball in his basket, then reached down into the water for more mud. I squatted down beside him, and began to make balls of mud also.

"This mud is good for young mothers," he said "it makes them strong."

We filled our baskets with the wet balls, and walked back where we left our large baskets. Konani had not returned. We sat, drank water and rested.

"You will be a good medicine man," the holy man told me, "you have traveled, and learned much as a boy."

"I have learned much." I said, and smiled.

"You like to learn." he said.

I nodded, "I am happy to learn from you."

"Your teacher speaks to you?" he asked me.

"Yes" I answered.

He nodded, "Good, she will teach you also."

Konani walked to us, with a basket in his hand, and he smiled. "Eggs."

The holy man looked into Konani's basket, and smiled.

"We will have a fire pit on the sand this night, and eat these." the holy man said.

I was glad to know that we would sleep by the water, and listen to the waves. Konani packed the balls of mud into his, and the holy man's large baskets, then gave me his basket with the eggs. I looked into it, and saw little eggs with spots on them.

"Don't break those!"

He picked a large handful of grass, and packed it around the eggs so they did not touch each other, then covered them until they were hidden.

"Good." he said.

We left the clearing, and traveled down the trail toward the sea. With every step, I was glad to leave the mountain. Now I saw the line of water peeking through the trees, and walked faster behind Konani.

He looked over his shoulder, "Do you want to pass me?'

"No!" I laughed, "the water pulls me to her!"

"I am glad to leave this mountain also."


WE STOOD ON A CLIFF, looking down on the sand, and water. I watched the waves roll in, felt the wind blowing up to us, and breathed the air. Many big rocks lie under the water.

"This is not good for boats." I said.

Konani nodded, "It will keep the chief's son away."

Far away, clouds hung over the sea, and the sun traveled down behind them. I wondered if Kekoa and the villagers were now safely on a new island, and if their travel over the water was good. I thought of Milana, she looked small in the boat when she left,

"I will fish." Konani said.

"Fish and eggs!" the holy man cried out.

"We will feast!" Konani said.

We climbed down the cliff and started to work. I gathered dry wood, and the holy man built a fire pit in the sand.

"Watch the fire." he told me, and left.

I watched him walk down the sand, then to the water, and pull up sea plants. Konani returned with fish, wrapped the fish and eggs in palms leaves, to lay by the hot fire. The holy man returned, piled the sea plants on the palm leaves, and the hot fire made their water rise into the air. Konani left again, to cut shells, from the rocks under the water. These shells also grew by my village, and I liked them.

"I CANNOT EAT MORE!" I cried out, made a face, and rolled on my side laughing.

The holy man and Konani also laughed. When the fish, eggs, shells and sea plants came off the fire, they tasted delicious, and we had all eaten until our bellies were full. The holy man stood up, rubbed his belly and grabbed his bedroll. Konani stood up also, and I watched them lay their bed rolls out by the fire pit.

"I will sleep good!" Konani said.

I did not stand. I crawled on my hands and legs to my bedroll, and they laughed.

"You cannot walk?" Konani asked.

"My belly is too full." I said.

"We will not feast again!" the holy man told us.

I jumped to my feet, and grabbed my bedroll. "I am good! We can feast!"

They laughed loudly, and watched me spread out my bedroll, across the fire from them.

"Good," Konani said, "I will cut shells from the rocks, to eat when we wake."

"I will fish." I told them.

"Your bones are growing!" The holy man said, and smiled at me.

I lay down, put my arms behind my head, and looked up into the dark sky. I saw a small moon, and many bright lights around it. I closed my eyes, listened to the waves, and soon heard no more.

# CHAPTER 8

*K*onani cut shells from the rocks, and I used my blade to spear a fish. The holy man put the tea pot in the fire pit, and was ready to eat when we returned.

"Eat quickly." he told us, "water clouds come."

I looked across the sea, and saw a small line of dark over the water. They were far away, then turned to watch the shells get hot, and open up. Konani pulled them from the fire, they tasted like the sea water, and we ate them with the fish. We sipped our tea, when I saw a man walking toward us on the sand. I pointed to him. Konani, and the holy man, turned to look. When he got closer, I saw he also carried a large basket on his back. He wore no sandals, and a cloth hung from his waist.

The holy man stood, "Welcome."

The man nodded, and looked at us.

"Tea?" the holy man asked.

"Thank you," he said, and sat down by Konani.

"I am Maleko."

"Do you live on the flat land?" the holy man asked.

"Yes"

The holy man gave Maleko tea in his shell.

Maleko took the tea, and sipped it.

Maleko told us he had joined with a woman on the flat lands, and they had a family.

"Is your father and mother there?"

He nodded, "They brought me here, after a battle on our old island."

"You were young?"

"No, I was wounded, and we left on our boat."

"Did you know Kekoa?" the holy man asked.

"Yes." Maleko said, "He fought also, and I did not know if he passed."

The holy man told Maleko of Kekoa coming to this island with many wounds.

Maleko nodded, and showed us his arm, with a long mark.

"He joined with a woman, and has a family." the holy man said, then told him of the chief's son, and Kekoa guiding the villagers on boats to a new island.

"Will these warriors come to the flat land?" Maleko asked.

The holy man shook his head, "I do not know, yet the villages must be prepared."

Maleko and the holy man talked of this, Konani poked me and pointed to the water. We got up, and walked away.

"Where is your village?" I asked Konani.

"On the flat land." He answered.

"Where does the holy man come from?" I wanted to know.

"The flat land."

"Did you know him as a child?" I asked.

"No, the flat land is large, with many villages. I saw him when he traveled, and gave medicine, yet I did not know him."

We climbed on rocks that went into the water, sat down, and watched the waves crash against them.

"I am glad my village is by the water." I said.

"Yes, it gives us much."

"Konani! Kai!" the holy man called to us, and waved us back.

"We leave!" Konani said, and we ran back.

. . .

WE WALKED along the water following Maleko, and gathered long sea plants, that washed up on the sand. I had eaten this plant in my village, and the holy man told us we would use it for medicine. I felt cold wind blowing from the water, and looked to see low dark clouds.

"Water will fall soon." Maleko said, and pointed to them.

The holy man also looked, "Walk fast!" he told us.

Maleko and the holy man took long steps, and walked quickly ahead. We followed, and had traveled far along the water, when the dark clouds blew over us. The cold wind blew stronger and stronger, and I reached up to hold my basket tightly.

The wind pushed big waves toward the sand where we walked, so we moved away from the water, walking below the cliff. I looked again and again, over my shoulder, at the waves coming closer. The winds carried much water, it hit us on the head and bodies. The water blew into my eyes, and it was hard to see. My skin was cold, and my body started to shake.

The water got louder, I heard the big waves crashing close, yet tried to see where Konani went ahead of me. I felt water rushing over my feet and legs, then it crashed against the cliff and moved back over my legs to the sea. I dug my feet into the sand, so I would not fall, then pulled my feet up out of the sand and began to walk.

I heard a loud crash, and turned to see a large wave pushing water toward me. I looked at Konani, saw him running in the water ahead of me, then the water rushed over my legs and crashed into the cliff. I tried to run, yet when the water moved back from the cliff, it pulled me with it and I fell on my knees. I pushed hard on the sand, stood up, and started to run.

I saw Maleko climbing up rocks, that went up the cliff, and the holy man climbed behind him. I tried to run, yet the water pulled at me, and it was hard to move with the basket on my back. I heard another wave crash, and I looked to see a big wave coming in.

"Kai!" Konani yelled.

He stood on the rocks, "Kai! Run!"

I pulled my foot up from the water and leaped out with a big jump, then fought the water to go to him. I reached the rocks, he grabbed my basket, and lifted me with it to where he stood. Water crashed on the rocks, and hit the back of my legs. Konani still held my basket and I looked down, to see the water was fierce and deep behind me.

My legs shook, and I looked up at Konani. "Thank you."

WE CLIMBED up the wet rocks, and the wind blew hard with water on our backs. Maleko and the holy man waited at the top of the cliff, watching us. Konani and I reached them and stopped, my body was shaking, and my teeth made noises.

Maleko looked at the holy man, "Do you want a fire?"

The holy man shook his head, and lifted the basket from my back. Konani pulled the wet blanket off, and the wind hit my back making me shake harder. The holy man took the blanket from inside his bedroll, and wrapped it around me. It was dry, and felt warm on my skin. Then he put my wet blanket in my basket, and held it. Water still fell on my head, yet my body did not shake as hard.

"We are ready." he told Maleko.

Maleko looked at me, then turned to walk along the cliff. The wind blew hard, and the water fell on us, yet I was glad to be away from the waves.

THE CLOUDS BLEW PAST US, and now I saw clear sky over the sea. I was wet, yet as I walked, my body warmed. I walked past Konani to the holy man.

"Thank you." I told the holy man, and took my basket from his arm.

Maleko led us from the cliff back down to the sand. I looked ahead and saw sand along the water, so far that I did not see an end. The mountains did not come down close to the water here, the mountains were far away. and this flat land traveled back slowly climbing up to the mountains. I had not seen such a place as this, it was large and flat, and I knew why many villages were built here.

I STARTED TO SEE HUTS, many huts. These villagers had fruit trees and plants growing around their huts, they had carried their boats up away from the water, and laid them on the dirt.

"Why are the boats on land?" I asked.

"The night water comes up here." Konani said, and waved his hand to the area where we walked.

Maleko stopped, "I go there." and he pointed to a long trail that led into the mountains, "You are welcome at my hut."

"Thank you." the holy man said, "We go to my family."

"Travel well." Maleko told us, and walked away.

We walked on a trail that led us across the flat land, and slowly away from the water. We passed huts, and the villagers waved. The trail was well used, and I thought there were many travelers that walked here. The holy man led us to huts that were built around a fire pit.

"My brothers' huts." he said.

I saw women working, children playing, and men that sat talking by the fire pit. They looked up and watched us. The holy man waved to them, and they stood with big smiles.

"Akamu! they yelled.

The men ran to us, and grabbed the holy man, "Akamu!" The holy man laughed hard, as one of his brothers lifted him off the ground.

"Welcome brother!"

The children ran to him also, "Akamu!" they cried out, and the holy man bent down to each one. Now the women came, looking at us, and greeting the holy man.

"This is Konani and Kai " the holy man said.

"Welcome, I am Hiapo," his brother said, and pointed to the other brother, "this is Mano."

"Sit at the fire." Mano told us.

The holy man smiled, and was happy. We sat down with the men at the fire pit, and a brother put wood on the fire.

"Where are Aukai and Kanoa?" the holy man asked.

"They fish."

The women brought fish on palm leaves. The fish was cold and not cooked, it sat in fruit juice mixed with a plant. I bit into it, and it was good. The fish tasted sweet from the juice, yet the plant made my mouth burn. I ate my fish quickly, then looked around at the others still eating.

"He grows!" a brother said, and they laughed.

The brothers told the holy man of their families, and the holy man told them of the chief's son.

"Have their mother and father passed?" I whispered to Konani.

"Yes." Konani said, "A sickness took many villagers, their mother and father passed when he was a little boy."

"Sickness?" I said, thinking of the mountain people.

"Not like the mountain sickness," Konani told me.

I nodded, and was glad of this.

"Their grandmother and grandfather cared for them." Konani said, and looked past me.

I turned to see men walking to us, they smiled.

"Akamu!"

The holy man's other brothers had returned from fishing, and were happy to see him.

"Kai," the holy man called me, and pointed to a hut, "go there, and pick fruit."

I walked to the trees that grew by the hut, and saw many fruits. There were also many plants that grew there, and I saw leaves that we used for medicine. I picked fruit, returned to the fire pit, and gave the fruit away.

"I saw plants that we use for medicine." I said.

"When grandmother gathered plants for medicines, she pulled the plant from the dirt, and put them in the ground here." the holy man told me.

"Grandmother helped babies come in." Hiapo said, and cared for the sick."

"I went with her to gather plants, and she taught me to make medicine," the holy man said, "when she was old, I carried her basket, and took the medicine to the villagers."

"The villagers told the old holy man of Akamu." Mano said.

"Grandmother dreamed of him," the holy man said, "she told me he would come."

"When he came," Aukai said, "she was not ready for you to leave."

"She told the holy man to return after many big moons." another said.

"She told me to put many plants in the dirt by the hut," the holy man told us, "so she did not travel far to gather them for medicine."

"Did you want to go?" I asked him.

"I wanted to learn medicine," he said, "I did not want to leave grandmother, yet she said she dreamed I would go."

"When the old holy man returned, we had a feast," Kanoa told us, "Grandfather gave Akamu a sharp blade, and new sandals."

"We made him a basket for his back, and a water pouch."

"Grandmother gave me this." the holy man said, and held the rock that hung from his neck.

"She wore that rock," Hiapo said, "she said it spoke to her."

I looked at the holy man, "Does it speak to you?"

He smiled, and reached up to hold the rock, "I feel grandmother in it."

"Grandmother passed when Akamu was at the holy man's camp," Hiapo said, "she spoke his name when she left."

The holy man nodded, "I heard her, and knew she had passed."


WE SAT AT THE FIRE, ate more, and I heard many things of the holy man and his brothers. We laughed, and enjoyed the women and children also. The children sang old songs that I knew from my village, and the women wanted to find Konani a young woman to join with.

Konani shook his head, and laughed. "I am not ready!"

When the women began to take the children to sleep in the huts, a brother looked at the holy man.

"We will travel to the villages here," Kanoa said, "to tell them of the chief's son."

"We have many strong men on the flat lands." Mano told him, "we will prepare."

"We will watch the mountain trail," Aukai said, "and the sea trail."

The holy man nodded, "We will go to the mountains to gather plants."

"Can I stay here, and eat with your family?" Konani asked, and laughed.

The brothers laughed, and the holy man spoke, "You and Kai will eat all their fish!"

"When will you return?" asked a brother.

"After we fill our baskets."

"Good," Kanoa said, "we want you here."

"We will build you a hut." Aukai told him.

The holy man looked at them, "I will think on this."

"Give medicine to the villagers here." Kanoa said.

The holy man looked at his brothers, then at me and Konani. "We will return and stay."

The brothers were happy, and talked of building his hut.

"We will stay!" I thought. I liked the brothers who laughed much, and their women that gave us good food.


"WE WILL PREPARE OUR BASKETS." Konani told me.

Our baskets leaned against a hut, and I looked inside mine. The balls of mud were still wet at the bottom.

Konani looked at them, "Put those on a palm leaf for the holy man, and wash your basket with water so it is clean."

I placed the balls on a palm leaf, and walked to the sea with my basket. I looked along the long sand, saw many huts sitting back from the water, and more going up to the mountains. I stepped into the water, bent down to let a small wave run into my basket, then lifted it up and poured the water out. The mud ran out with the water. I put more water in my basket and poured it out, again and again, until the mud was washed away.

I stood up, let the water drip from my basket, and looked across the sea. I saw large fish jump together out of the water.

"They are big!"

I waited, and saw them again. They moved through the water quickly, and jumped from it into the air. I smiled, and wondered how they knew when the other would jump. Water washed over my feet, and I looked down to see a small shell by my foot. It had a hole at the top.

"I will put this on a string." I thought, and quickly picked it up, before the water washed it away.

A sea bird flew over my head, and cried loudly. I looked again at the sea, and felt the wind blow on my face. Peace came into my heart.

"The peace you feel," my teacher whispered, "is in the sea and sky. Also, the birds and fish."

I had not thought of this.

"This peace will not leave you." she said.

"I do not feel peace when I think of the chief's son," I told her, "and when my heart hurts for mother."

"It is there," she told me.

I shook my head, "Peace hides from me."

"Let your thoughts rest, peace will come."

I looked across the water, breathed in slowly, then let the air out. "I will think on this."

"Do not think," she said, and I felt her leave.

"Do not think!" "Let your thoughts rest!" I threw the shell back into the water, and grabbed my basket.

"I feel no peace now!" I said, and turned to go back.

I OPENED MY EYES, heard branches popping and burning in the fire pit. I turned over to see Konani, poking at the fire with a stick. The sun was not up, yet some light shone behind black clouds covering the sky. A cold wind blew from the water, and I pulled my blanket up to cover my ear. I heard the cry of a baby coming from one of the brother's huts, yet only Konani and I were at the fire pit. The holy man's bed roll was tied, and sat next to his basket. Konani had done the same. I pushed back my warm blanket, and felt the cold air blow on my skin.

"The sky will pour water." Konani told me.

"It is cold." I said, and rolled up my blanket.

I stood close to the fire, and watched Konani put the tea pot by the it. A man walked in the darkness, and as he came into the light of the fire, I saw it was the holy man.

"We will travel after tea." he said.

A brother came out of his hut, and walked to us, giving us dried fish and fresh fruit.

"The sky is not good for travel" he said, looking up.

"We will carry palm leaves to cover our heads." the holy man told him.

"I will give you fishing blankets." his brother said.

I knew of these fishing blankets. They were woven tightly from palm leaves, and father wore them when he fished under wet sky.

"Good." I thought, "Our heads will be dry."

We finished drinking our tea, and the holy man stood. The brothers brought the fishing blankets, and helped us hang them over our heads and baskets. They hung down and covered our bodies.

The holy man looked down at his fishing blanket, and nodded, "Good."

"Travel well." they told us.

Their women and the children looked from the huts, yet did not come out in the cold air.

Drops of water started to fall on us as we left, yet I was dry under the fishing blanket. Only my legs and feet were getting wet and cold.

"Mud!" Konani called back.

I looked down, mud covered the path, and it pushed up over my sandals to stick on my feet. We walked toward the mountains, and as we walked higher up the trail, more water fell on us. The sky was dark with the water clouds over our heads.

"Maleko's hut is on this trail." I thought, and wondered if we would see him. I saw a hut, and as we came closer, I heard voices inside.

The holy man stopped and yelled, "Maleko!"

An old man came to the doorway, and shook his head. He smiled, and I saw his teeth were gone in front.

"There." He pointed up the trail.

"Thank you." the holy man said, and we started walking.

The trail led us to another hut.

The holy man yelled again, "Maleko!"

A young woman came to the door, "He is there." and she pointed to the side of the hut.

We looked and saw Maleko, by a large pot, that caught the water running off the hut. He filled his tea pot with it.

"Welcome!" he said, seeing us.

Water poured from the sky on us.

"Come!" he said, "Come into my hut."

We took off our wet fishing blankets, and used to them cover our baskets, which we sat by the door. We took off our sandals, and washed our feet in the water running off the hut, before we stepped in. The hut was warm. A small fire pit burned wood in the center, and Maleko's woman sat in a corner weaving a basket, while his daughters made necklaces with shells.

Maleko spoke to his family, "This is the holy man I met," then he looked at us, "this is Konani and" he shook his head.

"Kai" I said, and his daughters laughed.

There were many girls, some young and others older, like Konani.

"Give them fish and fruit." Maleko told them. We sat on mats, and the daughters brought us hot fish they had cooked on the fire.

Maleko put the pot on the fire, "Hot tea will taste good."

We ate, and my belly was full.

"Thank you." I told them.

An older daughter walked to Konani, "Do you want a necklace?"

He looked at the holy man, who nodded at him.

"Yes" he said.

"Pick what you want." she told him, and walked back to sit by her sisters.

Konani stood, and went to her.

"Sit," she said, "I am Leilani."

He sat next to her, and began to look at the necklaces.

Maleko looked at me, "Do you want a necklace?"

I shook my head, "Not now."

The holy man told Maleko of his brothers.

"I have seen them." Maleko said, "I know where their huts are."

"If the chief's son comes," the holy man told him, "take your family there. My brothers will help protect them."

Maleko nodded, "I will tell my family to run there."

"Are there many huts on this trail?"

"No more," Maleko said, "My hut, and my mother and father live below."

"Tell them to prepare to leave." the holy man said.

"I do not want to fight," Maleko said, "yet I will protect my family."


I WATCHED KONANI LAUGH, and talk with the girls. Leilani smiled much at him, and Konani smiled also.

"He likes this girl." I thought.

Maleko's wife stood, and clapped her hands, "Get the tea."

The girls put down the necklaces, and got up. Leilani put her hand on Konani's shoulder as she stood, and smiled at him. He smiled at her, then looked at me. His eyes were happy.

The daughters gave us tea, I listened to the wind blow the water hard against the hut, and cold air blew past a woven mat hung in the doorway. Maleko and the holy man talked long of protecting the villages, and Konani made a necklace, with much help from Leilani.

I sat by the fire and was glad to be warm. I thought of mother, and my sisters in our hut, weaving mats and making necklaces. Maleko stood and walked to the doorway, looked out at the dark sky, and the water that still fell.

"Sleep here," Maleko told the holy man.

"Yes" the holy man said. "I do not want to travel now."

I looked to Konani, and he had not heard what the holy man said. He sat next to the Leilani, looking into her eyes talking. She listened, then laughed, and he laughed with her.

"He will join with her." my teacher whispered.

"He said he is not ready." I thought.

"His heart has joined with her." she said.

I watched them carefully, and wondered when my heart would join with a young woman such as this.

WE SLEPT on mats across the floor, and our shoulders touched. I was close to the fire pit, and felt it warm on my arm. I closed my eyes, and listened to the water falling on the hut. I took air in slowly, let my thoughts rest, and soon the peace before sleep came to me.

"Is this the peace?" I thought, "that comes when I do not think."

"You also felt this peace sitting by the waterfall." my teacher whispered.

KONANI SHOOK MY SHOULDER, and I woke up. Maleko and the holy man were already outside standing by the fire pit, and the daughters worked rolling up blankets, and getting food from baskets. I rolled up my bedroll, and tied it with the string. Konani stood by me, watching Leilani.

"I am ready." I told Konani.

He looked away from her, and walked outside. I followed him, happy to see a clear sky, and feel the sun on my face. I looked at the mountain, and the dark clouds still hung there.

"Are you ready?' the holy man said, and looked at Konani.

Konani nodded, and looked down. The holy man watched him, and said, "Come."

I started to follow them, when the holy man turned, and held up his hand.

"No," he said, "wait here."

The holy man turned, put his arm on Konani's shoulder, and they walked away. I heard the holy man speaking quietly, and I wondered what he said.

Maleko looked at me, and smiled, "You make medicine?"

THE FISH WAS COOKED, and the tea was ready to drink, when the holy man and Konani returned. Konani smiled at me, then his eyes looked for Maleko's daughter, who was inside the hut. Soon Maleko's woman and daughters walked out of the hut, and gave us palm leaves for our hot fish, and we ate while standing around the fire pit. Leilani stood across the fire pit from Konani, and they looked at each other. When we were finished, we put on our baskets.

"Thank you." the holy man told Maleko.

"Travel well."

The holy man walked away, and I waited for Konani. He put his basket on, and looked at Leilani. He smiled at her, and she smiled back. I looked at Maleko, and his woman, watch Konani with their daughter. I knew they saw what I did. Konani walked away and I followed, then he turned his head to look back as we left.

# CHAPTER 9

"We look for plants that only grow on this mountain." the holy man told me.

I was glad to see new plants, and make new medicines with them.

"Have you gathered plants here." I called to Konani.

"I have not seen them all."

The sun had been shining, and the sky was clear, when we left Maleko's hut. Yet, as we traveled up the trail into the mountain, I saw dark clouds hanging over us. Thick bushes grew above the trail, and below, the ground dropped down to a stream. Roots from trees, and rocks, made the trail hard to walk. We carefully put our feet down, so we would not fall, or slip down to the stream. Water started to fall, we had left the fishing blankets at Maleko's hut, and I did not want to be cold and wet again. My feet stepped down into mud on the trail, and I wondered if the holy man would keep going.

"Listen" he called back.

I heard branches snapping, and bushes moving.

"Run!" the holy man yelled.

I turned, and started to run, still watching where I put my feet.

"Ohhhhhh," I heard the holy man scream, and the sound of him falling.

I looked back, saw lots of water and mud filling the stream, and running over the trail. The mud and water hit Konani's legs, he fell, and slid into me. I was knocked down, and slid off the trail toward the stream. I landed on my basket, and as the water pushed me, my basket caught on a bush and I grabbed it to stop moving. The water was cold underneath me, I pulled myself up out of it and looked up. The holy man held on to tree branches, and stood on the trail.

"Climb!" he yelled.

I grabbed at bushes to climb up, and he bent down to grab my hand. I stepped up next to him, and looked at us. We were covered in mud.

"Konani!" the holy man yelled.

I looked down the trail, and saw him. He lay on the trail, not moving.

"Konani!" I called, and he did not answer.

The holy man grabbed bushes, and stepped carefully down the muddy trail to him. I followed, and saw Konani's leg had a large cut. He lay on his basket, with his head turned away. He did not move.

"Konani" the holy man yelled, and shook his shoulder.

"Ohh" he cried out, and tried to lift his head. The holy man squatted down at Konani's head.

"Where is your pain?" he asked Konani.

"My head" Konani answered, put his hands on his head, then he turned his face to me.

I saw a big bump, and cut on the side of his face.

"I fell on a rock" he said.

The holy man took off his basket, and pulled out a pouch.

"Ohhh!" Konani cried, when the holy man pressed dried leaves into the cut on his leg. The holy man reached up, and put leaves into the cut on his face.

"Sit up." the holy man said.

Konani pushed with his arms to sit, and I slipped the basket off his shoulders.

The holy man looked into Konani's face, "Can you stand?"

Konani leaned forward and put his good leg under him, grabbed the holy man's hand, and pulled himself up to stand. His eyes began to close, he started to fall again, and the holy man pulled him up.

"Konani" the holy man yelled, and shook his shoulders.

Konani's eyes opened, and he looked at me, yet his eyes did not shine. The holy man stood next to him, and put Konani's arm over his shoulder. Then the holy man put his own arm around Konani's waist.

"Lean on me, we will walk back." the holy man said.

Konani nodded.

I grabbed their baskets, and walked slowly behind them. I saw red water drip from the back of Konani's leg, and he tried not to step on it, when he walked. I looked at the holy man's legs, and they also had scratches and small cuts from the fall.


"YOU WERE STOPPED." I heard my teacher say, and saw a picture in my head of young men sitting at a fire pit. The men had black marks on their faces, and I knew it was the chief's son.

"Where does this trail go?" I asked the holy man.

"Through the mountains to the other side of the island."

"My teacher said we were stopped," I told him, "the chief's son, and his men, are on this trail."

The holy man was quiet, "You saw this?"

"Yes."

The holy man held up Konani as they walked. We traveled slow, and I wondered how far behind us the chief's son was. The holy man turned, and pulled Konani with him, to let me pass.

"Run to Maleko, warn him of the chief's son, and take his family to my brothers."

"I will come back." I told him.

"No," he shook his head, "do not return."

I looked at him, and did not want to leave.

"Run!" he yelled.

I slung the holy man's basket over one arm, and Konani's basket over the other, and ran down the trail. The baskets were hard to hold, and my feet slipped on the mud, yet I did not stop. The water stopped falling as I ran out of the mountain, so I ran faster.

I saw Maleko's daughters walking on the trail.

"Where is your father?"

"At the hut." they said, and I ran past them. They ran behind me.

"Maleko!" I yelled as I got closer to the hut. He walked out, and his woman and daughters also came out to see me.

He looked at the two baskets, "Where is the holy man? Where is Konani?"

"Konani has wounds, and the holy man helps him walk".

"I will help." Maleko said.

"No." I said, and sat down the baskets, "The chief's son comes."

Maleko looked at me, then at his woman.

"The holy man said leave!" I yelled, "go to his brothers, and he will bring Konani there."

Leilani started to shake, and water fell from her eyes. "I will help Konani."

Maleko yelled, "Help your mother!"

"Grab bedrolls and leave," he told his younger daughters, "run to your grandfather, and tell him to leave."

"Put fruit and fish in these." I said, and pointed to the baskets.

Maleko nodded, "Fill these."

His woman and daughters quickly filled the baskets, and put them on their backs.

"We leave!" Maleko called to his family, and we walked down the trail, where the grandmother and grandfather waited outside their hut.

"You carry a spear?" the grandfather asked when he saw Maleko.

"Yes."

"I have this" the grandfather held up a sharp blade used to cut big fish.

"Kai," Maleko said, "lead us."

I walked down the trail, and looked behind to see Maleko and his family. They traveled fast, and the grandfather and grandmother walked behind them.

I pointed down at the brother's huts, "There!"

The children saw us, then their mothers. "Kai," one asked, "where is Akamu?"

Then she looked at the others behind me, "They travel with you?"

I nodded, "The chief's son comes."

"Come!" she said, and took us to the fire pit, "the men fish."

The brothers' women and children joined Maleko, and his family there. They began to speak of the chief's son, and Leilani walked back to me.

"I do not see them." she said, looking up the trail going into the mountain.

The sun had dropped close to the water, and I also looked up the trail.

"They will come." I told her.


THE BROTHERS RETURNED FROM FISHING, and spoke with Maleko.

"We know where they travel." Maleko told them, "we will stop them on the trail."

"When the sun rises, the women and children will go to the old village," Kanoa said, "our family is there."

"I will gather men to fight." Aukai said.

"I will travel to the other villages." Mano said.

"Join us where the trail leads into the mountain." Maleko told them.

"Yes!" the brothers said, "we will gather there."

The women prepared fresh fish and fruit, and we stood waiting to eat.

"The ancestors are here," my teacher whispered.

I looked around the fire pit, and saw the faces of ancestors among the families.

"The ancestors will protect you."

I said nothing. "Say this." My teacher told me.

I started to speak, yet only a small sound came out. I took a breath, made fists, and shouted, "The ancestors are here!"

They stopped talking, and looked at me.

"The ancestors will protect you." I said.

"He sees the ancestors like our brother!" Kanoa said, and came to me.

Haipo came to me also, "Ask the ancestors to guide us."

I looked around, seeing their faces, and knew they needed to know this. I put my arms up, as the holy man did, and closed my eyes.

"Ancestors," I cried out, "guide us, and protect us in this battle."

Haipo slapped my back, and shouted out, "Yes!"

I opened my eyes, and Kanoa smiled at me. "Our brother has trained you well."

Darkness fell on us, yet the moon was big, and I watched the trail for the holy man and Konani. Leilani stood by me.

"Where are they?" she asked.

"They travel slow." I told her.

We watched, then Maleko came for her. "Come, you leave when the sun rises."

She started to speak, then did not, and followed her father back to sleep with her family.

THE SUN ROSE, and I watched the brothers lead their families, and Maleko's family away. The women walked slowly with small children, and the old grandfather and grandmother walked behind them.

"Thank you ancestors," I thought, "for guiding us."

I also watched the mountain trail for the holy man and Konani.

"They slept on the mountain." I thought, and wondered if Konani needed medicine.

"I will go!" I grabbed the holy man's basket, and started up the trail.

I walked to Maleko's hut, and looked up to where the trail led into the mountain. I saw a man sitting next to the trail. I looked hard, "The holy man?"

I ran now, and soon saw him. The holy man sat by the trail, and Konani lay next to him, with his eyes closed. I ran to them, and dropped down to the dirt.

"Has he passed?"

Konani opened his eyes, looked at me, yet did not speak.

"He rested." the holy man said.

The holy man grabbed his basket, and slipped it off my shoulders. He dug inside, and pulled tea leaves out.

"Chew." he said, and put some in Konani's mouth. Then he pulled out the pouch, with medicine for his wounds. I watched as the holy man pressed more dried leaves into Konani's leg wound.

"Your brothers have left with the families," I told them, "and will bring men to gather here."

The holy man listened, and put medicine in the cut on Konani's head.

"Maleko said they will stop the chief's son here."

The holy man looked up the trail, where it went into the mountain, and handed me the pouch.

"We leave." he said, and gave his basket to me.

The holy man helped Konani to stand, and we started to walk. The trail no longer had roots and rocks to step over, yet Konani walked slow. We passed Maleko's hut, and I looked up the trail, not wanting to see the chief's son and his warriors. Then we reached the grandparents hut, and the holy man stopped to look at Konani.

"Do you need to rest?" he asked.

Konani shook his head, I saw his face was pale with pain, and he looked tired. I let the holy man and Konani walk in front of me, and while I followed, I looked over my shoulder much to watch the trail behind us. We reached his brother's fire pit, and the holy man took Konani into his brother's hut.

"I am glad to stop." Konani said.

"Kai," the holy man said, "bring water."

I walked outside, found a pot of water to bring back, and sat it near the holy man.

"Do you want fruit?" I asked.

"I want sleep." Konani said.

The holy man washed Konani leg, and pressed more leaves into the wound.

"It will heal" he told Konani.

I looked at Konani, whose eyes were tired.

"Sleep." the holy man said, and Konani lay down on his back. "Ohhh." he said, and slowly rolled to his side.

The holy man stood up, and his legs made noise, "My bones hurt."

I followed him out to the fire pit, the holy man ate fruit, and rested.

"I am glad you are safe." I told him.

"I thank the ancestors." he said, and nodded.

The holy man and I slept in the hut with Konani. I awoke many times thinking of the battle.

"Protect the men," I asked the ancestors, "help them stop the chief's son."

I AWOKE AGAIN, and now the sun shined brightly outside. Konani slept, yet the holy man was gone. I rubbed my eyes, and quietly got up. Konani breathed easy, so I walked out and looked to the fire pit, where the holy man sat drinking tea. He pointed to the tea pot by the fire.

"Thank you" I said, and poured some.

"I will leave to join my brothers, you stay and care for Konani." he told me.

"Yes."

"We will..." the holy man stopped speaking, and turned to look behind him.

Walking fast this way was Maleko, and Leilani. They walked to us, and his daughter looked around.

"Where is Konani?"

The holy man pointed to the hut, "There."

She walked quickly to the hut, and went inside.

"She would not stay in the old village," Maleko said, and shrugged his shoulders, "She wants to care for him."

The holy man nodded, "She will help Kai."

"She wants to join with Konani." Maleko said.

"I have seen this." the holy man said, "Konani wants to join with her also."

Maleko looked at the holy man, "Konani will be a good son."

The holy nodded, "Are you ready to leave?"

Maleko walked to the hut, and saw his daughter standing over Konani, who slept.

"We go." he told her, she walked over and wrapped her arms around him.

"Be safe." she said, with water in her eyes.

Maleko held her shoulders, and looked in her eyes, "I will return."

"He will return," the holy man told her, as we stepped into the hut.

He looked at Konani, then at her, "Make tea, give him fruit and fish."

Maleko hit the long spear to the ground, and said, "I am ready."

Maleko looked at Leilani, then walked outside.

The holy man looked at me, "Clean his wounds, and put medicine on them."

"Be safe." I told him.

He grabbed his medicine basket, and walked out.

I looked at Konani, he was now awake, and looked at Leilani.

"She will care for you." I said, and walked out.

I went behind the hut, looked up to the mountain, and watched the holy man and Maleko walking up the trail. I knew that I would not see the battle from here.

"The brothers are strong," I thought, and they are gathering others to fight. I wondered what I would do if I saw the chief's son coming down the trail.

"We will go to the fishing boat," I thought, "and leave."

I sat down, and leaned against the hut, "I will watch the trail."

I sat and watched, the clouds had blown away, and the sky was clear. I heard voices and laughter from the hut, I watched birds fly, and my eyes grew tired. "I did not sleep good." I thought, and let my eyes close.

. . .

MY HEAD JERKED UP, I had fallen asleep. I looked up the trail, did not see men, then I walked around to the doorway of the hut. Leilani sat on the floor next to Konani, with her hand on his arm.

"Kai" he called to me.

"You have not passed to be with the ancestors?" I asked.

Leilani shook her head, "I will chase away the ancestors, if they try to take Konani!"

Konani laughed, "Come in."

"I watch the trail" I said, "she watches you."

"She cares for me well." he said, and looked at her.

I walked back around the hut to a fruit tree, grabbed a piece of fruit, and sat down by the hut.


THE SUN CAME from behind the mountains, traveled over the brothers' hut, then dropped down close to the water. I had cleaned Konani's wounds, pressed medicine into them, and now sat by the hut again. My belly was hungry, and I thought of walking into the hut, when I heard footsteps.

"Here," Leilani gave me dried fish.

I took it, happy to eat. "Is he good?"

"He sleeps."

"I am glad you are here," I told her.

She smiled at me, "I am also." Then turned, and walked back into the hut.

I ate the fish, and picked more fruit from the tree. I looked to the sea, and the sun was ready to go behind the water.

"My bedroll." I thought.

"You sleep outside?" Konani asked, as I grabbed my bedroll.

I nodded, "I will watch." I told him, "If the chief's son comes, we will leave in a boat."

"Yes." Konani said.

"I have to warn my mother." Leilani said, and looked at Konani.

"Yes, " Konani said softly, "we will warn your mother."

I looked at them, and thought, "They will join."

I left them, walked behind the hut, and spread out my bed roll. Sitting down on it I strained to see the trail as darkness fell.

I AWOKE FEELING my leg being poked. I opened my eyes, and saw the trail clearly with the sunlight! I sat up quickly.

"Keeping watch?" Konani said, standing over me.

"You walk?"

He nodded, "I walk like an old man, and my head hurts."

"I will make you tea."

"Leilani made tea."

I stood up, "Are they back?"

"No."

"I will watch." I told him.

"You watch on your back!" he said, and laughed.

I shook my head, and laughed also.

Leilani came to us, with dried fish and tea.

"Eat." she told me.

Konani smiled at her, and looked back at me, "We will join when they return."

"I have heard this." I said, and smiled.

They were happy, they smiled, and laughed much. I wondered if I would feel this with a woman. I finished my fish and tea.

"Thank you Leilani."

"Konani told me you are his brother," she said, "you are my brother also."

"I have a new sister!" I told her.

I WATCHED AGAIN, and the sun traveled over my head to the sea. Darkness was falling when I saw men on the trail. I squeezed my eyes to see if they wore feathers on their heads, yet saw none.

"Konani! Konani!" I yelled.

Konani and Leilani came out of the hut to stand by me, and we looked far up the trail at the men walking.

"The holy man?" Konani asked.

"Is it my father?" Leilani cried out.

We watched them, and did not know who they were.

"Prepare to leave!" I told Leilani, "if we do not know these men, we go."

She ran into the hut, and soon came back, with bedrolls and baskets. The men slowly moved down the trail, and I thought I heard a shout.

I looked at Konani, "I cannot see them." he told me.

We watched, ready to leave, and then I saw a man walking with a tall spear.

"Maleko?"

Leilani looked, "My father!" She dropped the bedrolls and baskets, then ran to meet her father.

"She runs fast!" Konani said.

We heard the men shout out to Leilani as she ran to them, and saw her wrap her arms around her father. Konani and I waited by the huts, and watched them come closer.

"We need food!" Haipo called.

"and water!" Mano yelled.

I ran to get these, and the men went to stand around the fire pit.

A man I had not seen, and the holy man, helped Aukai walk to sit by the fire pit.

Leilani gave the men fruit and water, and I looked at Aukai's wound. The thick part of his leg had a large cut, and the holy man put medicine on it. There were many men from the flat lands with wounds, yet they would heal. They spoke of surprising the chief's son and his men.

"We waited in the bushes by the trail, where only one man can walk."

"Aukai walked up the trail to look for the chief's son," Kanoa said, "then ran down shouting!"

"His leg was cut!"

"I saw a spear flying through the air, and I turned away," Aukai said, "it flew to the ground next to me, and cut my leg as it passed!"

"Good that you run fast" a man said, and the men laughed loudly.

"They ran behind me!"

"We were ready for them!" a man said.

""I speared the first" a man called.

"They ran fast down the trail, and they fell on each other as we attacked."

"Others saw this, turned around, and ran away from us."

"We ran after them on the trail, I speared one, yet he did not stop."

"Did many pass to the ancestors?" Konani asked.

"Yes."

"Where are the bodies?" I asked.

"Akamu told us to put them under palm leaves and rocks."

"He told them to go back to their ancestors." A man said.

"They will not return to the flat lands!" a brother shouted, the men also shouted, and talked more of the battle.

Leilani stood by her father, and Konani stood next to her.

The holy man looked at me, "Konani heals."

"He was well cared for." I said, and looked at Leilani.

When the men finished eating, and talking of the battle, they left to join their families. The big moon gave them light, to walk in the darkness.

"Come," Maleko said to his daughter, "we talk to your mother."

Leilani smiled at Konani.

Maleko looked at Konani, "We will speak when I return."


THE ANCESTORS GUIDED Konani to Leilani. He said he was not ready, yet when he saw her, it was not hard for him to think of joining with her.

"I will build a hut here," he told me, "and we will have a family."

He was happy, and I was happy with him.

"She has many sisters!" he told me.

"No! I am not ready!" I cried out, and we laughed.

"The ancestors guide you also," my teacher whispered, "when you are ready, you will find a woman."

. . .

THE SUN ROSE, and we stood around the fire pit.

"We will fish," Kanoa said, "when our women return, we will feast!"

"Yes!" his brothers called out.

Aukai sat next to the holy man. "I will drink tea!" he told them as they left. The brothers laughed, and carried their boat to the water.

"Kai!" the holy man called to me, "gather wood for the fire, we will thank the ancestors this night!"

# CHAPTER 10

$\approx$

Maleko returned with his wife and daughters. The grandfather and grandmother, the brothers' women and children also returned, and laughter was heard around the fire pit. I piled wood in the fire pit for a great fire, the brothers caught many fish to cook for the feast, and the women prepared them.

Maleko walked with Konani down to the water, and Leilani watched them go. When Maleko and Konani returned, Leilani walked to them, and Maleko put his arms around her. They came back to the fire pit.

"We will feast for my new son!" yelled Maleko.

The men yelled out, and slapped Konani's back. The women gathered around Leilani, and they were happy. Konani walked to me and the holy man.

"I will build a hut, then we will join." he told us.

"We will help you!"

We feasted and laughed much. The children ran, and the young boys played at fighting, such as their fathers had done.

"I will build a hut there." Konani said, and pointed between the grandfather's hut, and the brothers' huts.

"I do not want to be close to the mountain trail." he said.

"When the sun rises," Kanoa told the others, "we will help Konani build a hut."

We cut down small trees, branches and palm leaves. The men worked together, knowing how to build a good hut, and singing as they did. Soon Leilani stood in front of her new hut.

"We will be dry and warm." she said, "I will weave mats for it."

Leilani, her mother and sisters wove mats, the brothers' women made baskets, and when the sun rose again, the holy man's brothers built another hut close to theirs.

"Akamu," Kanoa said, "you will sit at our fire pit."

He looked at me, "This is your hut also.

"Thank you." I said, and was happy that I had a new village, with the holy man and Konani.

With the huts built, a feast was planned to join Konani and Leilani. Kanoa and Mano carried their boat out to fish, and the holy man cared for Aukai's leg.

"It heals well." I said, seeing the long wound on the skin.

The holy man filled the cut with leaves, that he gathered by his grandmother's hut. The holy man had been teaching me about the plants that grew beside her hut, and how his grandmother used each one for medicine.

"We will travel after the feast" he told me.

"Where?"

"To your village, and the village with the grandfathers."

"Good," I told him, "I want to know if the chief's son hurt them."

The holy man nodded, "We will leave after the joining."


THE DAY WAS HERE to join Konani and Leilani. The sun was happy in the blue sky. Small white clouds came to see the ceremony, and the wind that blew from the sea was warm, and felt good on our skin.

We stood around the fire pit, and watched Konani and Leilani hold hands. Maleko stood next to Konani, and his woman next to Leilani. The holy man raised his arms into the sky,

"Thank you Father for this day, and thank you Mother for feeding us. Ancestors we ask you to join us for this feast. Konani is a man, with his own hut, and Leilani will be his woman." The holy man closed his eyes, and we watched him closely. He took a lot of air in, and breathed it out.

"Bless Konani and Leilani with many children, and much laughter." He opened his eyes and put a necklace of shells, and another of flowers over Konani's head and then Leilani's. He grabbed their hands, and wrapped another necklace of flowers around them.

"Konani and Leilani are joined."

I felt my heart warm, and I was happy for them. The holy man wrapped his arms around Konani and Leilani, then said, "You will have a boy."

Konani threw his head back and laughed loud, Maleko was well pleased with this, and slapped Konani on the back. Women and men stepped forward to slap Konani on the back, kiss Leilani, and give them mats, fruit, and other things to fill their new hut. Maleko's woman gave Leilani a new blanket, and Maleko gave Konani a new fishing net.

"Thank you father" Konani said to Maleko.

"Wait." Maleko said, and walked behind Kanoa's hut. He returned with the long spear he used in battle.

"I brought this from my old island." Maleko said, and gave the spear to Konani.

Konani looked at it, "You give this to me?"

"You will watch over us now," he said, and pointed to his family, "I will be a grandfather soon!"

There was much laughter, and we started to eat. I sat down, and put many fish on my palm leaf.

"Welcome!" I heard Maleko say.

I looked up to see men that fought with Maleko, walking with their families, to join the feast. Their women brought fruit, and many things to give Leilani for her hut. We ate, the men talked again of the battle, and the women talked of babies. I watched, and was happy. I was glad that I would stay in this village.

. . .

THE SUN now slept behind the water, and a great fire burned in the fire pit. Kanoa walked from his hut, with the strong juice that we drink at feasts. He handed it to Konani.

"Go to your hut, and drink this with your woman."

The men laughed, "Yes," they called out, "go to your hut!"

Konani took the juice, and looked at Leilani.

"Come!" he said to Leilani, in a strong voice.

I laughed at this, I knew Konani tried to be a man.

We cheered, as Konani and Leilani walked to their new hut.

"We will find you a woman," Kanoa said looking at me, "Maleko has many daughters!"

"I do!" Maleko yelled.

"No!" I shook my head, "I am not ready!"

The men laughed, and clapped me on the back, and arms.

"I get more juice!" Kanoa said, and went back to his hut.

The holy man let women and children sleep in his hut, and we slept with the men around the fire pit.

When the sun rose, the holy man had pulled plants from dirt around his grandmother's hut.

"Your grandmother's medicine!" I said.

"We take it to Konani." he answered, and put them into our baskets.

Konani and Leilani stood outside their hut, and waved to us.

"We brought you plants," the holy man told them, "to grow for medicine."

"Thank you" Konani took the baskets from him.

We found an area where the dirt was soft, and put the plants in.

"You are the medicine man for the flat lands." the holy man told Konani.

"You will travel?" Konani asked.

"We will return to the other villages."

Leilani looked at the plants we put in the dirt, "I want fruit trees."

"Yes, this dirt is good," the holy man said, "I will bring back trees for you."

We sat and talked with Konani, then returned to the brothers' fire pit.

"We leave soon," the holy man told his brother.

"You have a hut when you return." Kanoa said.

"Thank you for my new hut," he told them, "I am glad to return."


THE HOLY MAN filled his basket with medicine, and told me, "Pick leaves from my grandmother's plants."

I gathered many leaves, putting them in pouches, then returned to the holy man.

"You carry those." He told me, "we will pick more as we travel."

We put on our baskets, and bedrolls, then walked to his brothers at the fire pit.

"Thank you," the holy man said, "we are ready."

Kanoa walked to him, and clapped him on the arm, "Travel well."

"Travel well." Aukai called to us.

We walked away, and I was glad to leave. I wanted to know if the chief's son had hurt my family, or other villagers on their way here. We came to Konani's hut and stopped. Konani hauled rocks to make a fire pit, and Leilani dug holes in the dirt for plants.

"Make medicine also," the holy man told him.

Konani dropped the rock down, and nodded, "I will."

"Do you want tea?" Leilani asked.

"No, we travel fast." the holy man said, "we will bring fruit trees, and tea back."

"Good." Konani smiled.

The holy man put his hand on Konani's shoulder, "Give medicine to the villagers, they will give you fish."

"I will." Konani said, "Travel well."


WE LEFT and walked by Leilani's grandfather, who waved, then up the trail to Maleko's hut. We did not stop, and Maleko and his family waved, as we passed. We walked up, closer to the mountain trail, and I looked for signs of the battle.

"The bodies." the holy man pointed to a pile, with palm leaves and rocks, "were there."

"Where are they?"

"The warriors returned in darkness, and buried them on the mountain."

He walked to the pile, put his basket down, and reached inside. He pulled out his feather, and the dried plants bound with string.

"We will bless this place." he said, "build a small fire."

I built a fire, he used it to burn the dried plants, then waved the smoke with the feather.

"Ancestors," he said, "give these men peace, and bring peace to the land."

He walked around the pile waving smoke, when he finished, he held the plant on the dirt until it stopped burning.

The holy man looked at me, "We go."


WE WALKED CAREFULLY along the trail, listening to the stream, and enjoyed the cool air under the trees. The holy man stopped, and we drank water from our pouches.

"We will sleep on the sand this night." the holy man said.

We ate dried fish, and picked fruit as we traveled. The trail took us away from the stream, and we climbed over rocks, to see a waterfall with a pool of water below it.

"We will not swim." the holy man told me, as we passed by.

The sun went behind the mountain, darkness was falling, and we walked faster. I wanted to see the sand, and hear the waves. I heard a sea bird cry, and knew that we were close, then I heard the water. The holy man stopped, and I walked beside him. We stood above the sand on a small cliff.

"We sleep there." the holy man pointed to where the sand was far from the sea, and rocks kept the water back.

We climbed down the cliff, and walked to the area. Then I saw a fire pit, and knew this was where the chief's son had also slept.

"Travelers sleep here." he told me.

I was happy to put down my basket and bed roll. "I am tired."

"No fire this night." the holy man said, and lay out his bed roll.

I lay on mine, listened to the waves, and thought of when Konani traveled with us.

"He walks a new path." my teacher whispered, and I closed my eyes to sleep.

I slept without moving, and awoke to mist on my face. I pulled my blanket up, to cover my neck, and looked to where the holy man slept. His bedroll was ready for travel, set next to the rocks, and he was gone. I closed my eyes, enjoyed the quiet, and felt myself drift into sleep.

"Ready?' the holy man said, and pushed my leg with his foot.

I opened my eyes, he stood above me.

"Yes."

WE TRAVELED FAST to my village. Children ran to us, and women waved. The sounds of a village came to us, and I knew my family was safe. I was happy to see my father and brothers at the fire pit, and we sat to talk.

"The grandmothers and grandfathers told the chief's son that the young had passed with sickness." My father said.

The holy man nodded, "Did he stay?"

My father laughed, "He left quickly!"

The holy man told them of the battle on the flat lands, we enjoyed fresh fish, and tea. When darkness came, a large fire burned.

The holy man stood, "Ancestors, we thank you for protecting this village."

The villagers shouted out, "Thank you!" "Thank you ancestors!"

"Join us now, walk with us to care for our children, and guide us to fish." The holy man called out.

The villagers were happy with this blessing, nodding their heads and talking amongst themselves. He sat down, and my brother brought the strong juice to the fire pit.

"Drink!" my brother said, and handed it to the holy man.

The holy man took a drink, passed it to my father, and he drank.

"We leave when the sun rises." The holy man told him.

"Thank you for returning," father said, "I am glad to know of the war birds."

Then father stood, "I am tired," he said, and looked at me, "travel well."

My brothers clapped me on the back, "Travel well."


THE SUN WAS NOT UP, yet it's light showed our way on the trail, as we left the village. We walked fast, and far along the water, when the sun came over our heads.

"You travel well." the holy man told me.

I was glad that I could carry my basket and bedroll, and stay behind him.

"We travel to the sea caves." he told me.

"The young father took his wife, and baby there" I said.

"Yes" the holy man said.

"Look" the holy man said, and pointed to a sea cave in the cliff above us.

We climbed up the dirt and rocks, to stand in front of the cave.

"They are gone."

We saw an old fire pit, and the dirt of the cave swept clean.

"They went back to their village." the holy man told me.

I looked around, and saw a trail that climbed to the top of the cliff.

"They climbed up to hide from the chief's son" I said, and pointed to the trail.

"Yes," he said, "they saw the chief's son far away on the sand, and left the cave safely."

"I am glad."

"We will sleep in their village" he said

We climbed up the cliff, and walked where the young family had. The trees and plants, that grew along the cliff, made a good place to hide from the chief's son.

"I will be glad to see the grandfathers again" the holy man said.

"I want to hear of the chief's son!" I told him.

As we walked along the top of the cliff, I thought of the young father and mother, traveling with their baby here. The cliff ended, and we climbed down large rocks to the sand. We passed another fire pit, and I wondered if the chief's son had stopped here also.

The sun was close to the water, when we saw the huts of the village. No children ran to us, and the village was quiet. We walked past huts that held no families, and my heart hurt for the villagers here. At the fire pit, we saw grandfathers and grandmothers, and I looked for Milana's grandfather. I found him, and sat down.

"Welcome." He said.

The holy man looked around at the old faces, "Tell me of the chief's son."

"He asked us, "Where are the young?" Milana's grandfather said, "We told him a great sickness took them."

"My village also said the young passed with sickness!" I told them.

Another grandfather said, "Many grandmothers still cried, and the warriors saw this."

Milana's grandfather said, "We told them the young that did not pass, took the boats and traveled on the sea."

The holy man nodded.

"He looked in the huts, and asked about the sickness," the grandfather leaned back, and looked at me, "we told him the wind carried the sickness to the young, while they slept."

The holy man laughed loud, "What did he say?"

The grandfather slapped his leg, "The chief's son told his warriors they would leave, and go far from our village."

"He feared our ancestors!" said another, and they all laughed

"We saw their fire pit on the sand." I said.

"They traveled to the flat lands, and there was a battle," the holy man told them, "the chief's son, and many men, passed to be with their ancestors."

"Did you capture the other warriors?" an old man asked.

"No," the holy man said, "they returned to their village."

"They did not return here." a grandfather said.

"They traveled quickly on the mountain trail." the holy man told them.

The holy man spoke with the villagers, and I left to find the young mother, that could not travel. She sat in her hut, weaving a mat, and her baby slept.

"He has many grandmothers!" she told me.

"Are you strong?" I asked.

"Yes," she said, and smiled.

"I will give you tea to make for the baby when he is sick and hot."

"Thank you."

I handed her a pouch with the tea leaves, and left. I returned to the fire pit, and sat with the holy man. A grandmother handed me a palm leaf, with fish on it. It was cold fish, not cooked on the fire, cut into pieces. The fish was mixed with fruit juice, and a plant that grows here. I grabbed a big piece with my fingers, put it in my mouth, and bit into it. The grandmother watched me, with a smile on her face.

"Ohhhh." I cried, my mouth was on fire. I bit into the fish again, and now my throat burned. Water came to my eyes, and I reached for my water pouch.

"My mouth is on fire!" I cried out.

The grandfathers and grandmothers laughed loud, and one grandfather slapped my back with his hand.

"She gave this to the chief's son also."

"I know why he left!" I said, while taking big drinks of water.

The holy man ate his, and smiled. "My grandmother made this for me."

The grandmother was happy, "It is the old way."


WE WALKED while the sun was up, and slept by the trail at night. I gave all the medicines in my basket to the grandfathers and grandmothers, and I was glad it was not heavy. The trail led us up, and around the top of the jagged mountains. We saw the sea around the island, yet did not hear it. There were no trees this high, and when the sun rose above us, we were hot. Water dripped down my face, and my body was also wet with water. I thought of the mountain river, with the deep pool, and knew I would swim when we reached camp.

The holy man did not speak, until we reached the waterfall. He turned to me, and asked, "Can you climb with your basket?"

I felt strong, and the basket was empty.

"Yes." I said, and followed him up between the rocks, then on the steps.

We reached the top, and I saw the river and the pool. I went to the water, put my basket down, and jumped into it. I swam, and watched the holy man go into camp, soon he walked back to me with a smile.

"The chief's son was not here." he said, "he traveled on the lower trail."

He was happy, and got into the water, still smiling. "I am happy to be back."

I washed my body, and enjoyed putting my head under the cool water. After we climbed out, he gathered wood for the fire, and I went to fish. When I returned to the camp, there was a fire in the pit, and the holy man had gathered leaves to eat with the fish.

"We feast!" I said.

"Yes, we celebrate this night," he said, "the ancestors are glad we have returned."

After eating, we sat at the fire pit drinking our tea. Darkness came into camp, and we enjoyed the fire. I was happy to be in the holy man's camp.

"This is my camp." I thought, and I felt peace here on the quiet mountain. I heard birds, and the sound of the river, as it flowed by.

"We will stay here many moons" the holy man said, "we will gather plants, and make medicine."

"I like it here." I told him.

The holy man was happy also, and after tea, he spoke to the ancestors.

"Thank you for watching over this camp."

I sat quietly, and watched him speak.

"Thank you for walking with us to the villages, and bringing us back here again."

In the darkness on the other side of the fire pit, I saw men standing,

"They are his teachers." I heard my teacher say.

"Those men?" I thought.

"I am not your only teacher." she said to me.

"Where are my other teachers?" I wondered.

"A medicine man will help," she said, "when you need him."

I heard the holy man breath in a lot of air, then blow it out, and looked at him.

He opened his eyes, and looked at me, "After we make medicine, we will go to Kekoa's old village"

"Will we be safe?" I asked, thinking of the men that followed the chief's son.

"The ancestors want us to make peace."

"Will Konani travel with us?"

"No, he cares for the villagers on the flat lands."

"I will travel now," the holy man said, "when I am old, I will stay in the hut near my brothers."

"Will I stay there also?"

"There," he said, "and here."

"I will travel to the villages?"

He looked at me, "Yes."

I smiled, "I will not leave this island?"

The holy man looked at me, did not speak, and I felt fear.

"Will you send me away?"

He shook his head, "I will not send you away."

# CHAPTER 11

*S*leep came easy in the peaceful old camp, and I awoke glad that the battle was over. I swept out my hut, and hung my bedroll in the sun. We wove new baskets, and cleaned out the food hut. I gathered, and stacked wood, for the fire pit.

"We can grow plants for medicine, and fruit trees, like your grandmother." I said.

The holy man looked at me, and nodded. I dug up the dirt, made an area to grow plants, and we found many plants and fruit trees to grow. After we packed the dirt down, I brought water from the river, and poured it around them.

The holy man put his hands over each plant, "Grow well." he said, then stood and looked at them.

"It was not my teacher's way to grow plants here," he told me, "I am glad you brought this to camp."

"Why did you not plant after your teacher passed?"

He shook his head, and laughed, "I do not know!"

I looked at him, and wondered, "He does not know?"

"He is a man." my teacher whispered.

I watched him walk away. I did not think of him as a man. He knew medicine, he spoke to the ancestors, and he was my teacher. He was honored by villages around the island, to me, he was above all men.

"He has learned much," my teacher said, "yet he still learns."

Her words came to me, and I knew then. He is a man, that has learned much, yet he is a man still learning. I saw him walking ahead of me, yet not above all others. I watched him gather strips of palm and sit down to weave.

"Thank you," I told my teacher.

WE SPENT our days gathering plants, making medicines, picking fruits and drying the fish we did not eat. We enjoyed our days, doing many things that made us happy. Camp was quiet except for sounds from the birds, water and trees. Every night the holy man spoke to the ancestors at the fire pit, and now when the ancestors spoke to him, I also heard their voices.

"You are ready to learn more," he told me, "go to the ceremony pool, sit and listen."

"What will I learn?"

"You will be given what you need."

When the sun rose, I walked to the ceremony pool, sat down and crossed my legs. When I was young, I sat like this by the water fall, and my teacher spoke to me then. I breathed in and heard the sounds of birds, then slowly breathed out with my eyes closed, and made my mind quiet. I looked into the darkness behind my eyes, and saw lights.

"We are with you." I heard a voice in my head say.

Then I saw myself on a long boat with others. I looked ahead, across the sea, and saw a small island. I heard a voice, a woman's voice say,

"Our village."

The vision went away, and I opened my eyes. I wiggled my toes and fingers, took a breath, and sat quietly.

"That young woman's voice," I thought, "I have heard it before."

I sat and waited for another vision, yet none came. I stood up, and wondered about the island I saw in my vision.

"I will ask the holy man." I thought.

I gathered plants and fruit as I walked back to camp. When I arrived, I saw the holy man sitting at the fire pit, speaking with a man and his son.

"This is Holokai, and his son." the holy man said, "Holokai has shown his son the mountain trail"

"Wecome." I told them, and sat down at the fire pit.

"The new chief did not follow his brother into battle," Holokai said, "he stayed in the village to protect the women and children."

The holy man nodded, "He is a good chief?"

"Yes," Holokai answered, "he told the men that returned from battle, they must join with a woman, and fish for the village."

"The men have done this?"

"They did not like the battle, and are happy to stay in the village."

"Good" the holy man said, "we will travel there."

Holokai nodded, "You are welcome in my village, I will tell the chief you come."


THEY SLEPT on their bedrolls in the traveler's hut, and sat drinking tea, after the sun rose.

"When the moon is big," the holy man said, "we will come."

We watched the father and son, walk down the trail, and the holy man turned to me, "We will prepare."

The holy man and I worked hard. Soon the food hut was filled with medicines, plants hanging to dry, and baskets of dried fish and fruit. We sat in the darkness next to the fire pit, I looked up into the night sky, and at the moon that was big.

"We travel soon?"

"We leave when the sun rises."

We filled our baskets with medicine, and I took our water pouches to the river. The holy man followed me, and walked into the water. He put his head under it, kicked his feet, and swam away.

I filled the pouches, then swam also. We enjoyed the river, and lay out in the sun to dry.

"I am ready." the holy man said, and stood up.

"I am ready." I told him, and was glad to travel to a village I had not seen.

THE HOLY MAN had taught me much. I learned of many plants, and how each plant was used. I learned which plants to dry and grind for medicines, and I learned which plants were used when freshly picked. I learned about other medicines made from mud, dried fish. and the bark of trees. The holy man also taught me to stay strong. He told me to swim every day until my body was tired, carry heavy baskets, and wood for the fire.

He also taught me to know when the ancestors guide us.

"Look for signs," he said, "then choose the path."

"A path?" I asked.

"The ancestors gave you a sign to leave your village." he told me.

"What was the sign?"

"They guided you out of your village to play," he said, "you enjoyed this more than fishing."

I nodded my head, "Yes."

"They prepared you to leave the village, and learn medicine."

"I did not know they guided me to play," I said, "yet my teacher spoke to me, by the waterfall."

"The ancestors speak to you in many ways," he said, "listen carefully."

I heard my teacher, yet now another voice talked to me, and it sounded like my own voice.

"What is this voice that speaks to me, and sounds like my own voice?" I asked him.

The holy man smiled, "Your highest teacher speaks with your heart, also the voice that sounds like your own."

"My heart?"

"Your head and heart speak often to you. When they speak of different paths, you will feel a battle inside."

"A battle?"

"When these voices battle," he said, "make your heart happy."

"What if I do not hear these voices, or listen to them?"

The holy man laughed, "They will make your path hard to walk, and when you are tired, you will let them lead."

I shook my head again, "I do not need all these voices!"

"The Great Father and Mother gave you these voices," he said, "they are a blessing."


WE LEFT THE OLD CAMP, and walked under the trees. The holy man told me of Kekoa, and how he came to live on our island.

"He was wounded from battle, and hot from the sickness in the wounds." he told me, "he was carried from the boat into a hut."

I shook my head, thinking of how many men would have to carry Kekoa.

"The marks from his wounds are big." I told him.

"A boy from the village came for me, and I took medicines and cared for him. A young woman helped me, and Kekoa joined with her after he healed."

We reached the trail. It was high on the mountain, and narrow. We walked on the side of a cliff, and I watched my feet carefully as I stepped. Konani had run on this trail in darkness, yet even with a full moon, I would be afraid to travel as he did.

"Konani was brave to run on this trail." I said.

"Yes, Konani, traveled well."

The trail now faced the sea. We stopped and looked ahead, the mountains rose up out of the water, without sand between.

"Where will we sleep?" I asked.

"On the trail."

Darkness was falling, and I kept my head down, looking where my feet stepped.

"There." the holy man said, and pointed ahead.

He stepped forward into a wider area of the trail, he turned around with his back to the mountain and sat down. He leaned against his basket, and stretched his legs out in front of him.

"We sleep here."

I looked at his feet hanging off the trail, thought of Holokai with his son, who also slept on the trail.

I turned with my back to the mountain, and sat down. I leaned against my basket, stretched out my legs, and it felt good to rest. We ate and looked at the sky.

"No clouds, this is good." the holy man said.

"Yes." I was glad there was no water making mud on the trail.

The holy man closed his eyes, and soon slept. I watched the night sky, full of lights, and saw one that flew quickly in front of me, then went back into the darkness.

"Where does it go?" I thought, then closed my eyes.

I felt the sea air blowing up from the water, and breathed in to smell it. My body was tired, and I soon traveled into the darkness of sleep.

THE HOLY MAN put a hand on my shoulder, and pushed himself up to stand.

"My bones hurt " he said, and laughed.

He put his hand out, and I grabbed it to stand. My legs were stiff, and I moved my feet to loosen them. The holy man took a drink of water from his pouch, and put dried fruit in his mouth. I did the same and we began to walk. The sky was clear, and I watched birds with their wings stretched out, letting the wind carry them.

The trail slowly traveled down, and my legs felt strong as I walked. I took bigger steps, to stay behind the holy man. Feeling good, I stretched my leg ahead, put my foot down, and felt my sandal slide on the dirt.

"Yeeaaww!" I screamed. I landed down on my bent leg, with the foot that slipped, stretched out in front of me. I put my hands down on the dirt, and did not move. The holy man turned quickly to see, held out his hand, and pulled me up.

"Take off your sandals." he told me.

I took my sandals off, and hung them from my basket. He also took off his sandals.

"Walk ahead," he said, "I will catch you if you fall."

He turned, stepped beside me, then was behind me.

"Are you ready?"

I nodded, started to walk, yet my legs were shaky.

Konani did not wear sandals when he ran into camp, now I knew, that is how he ran on the trail. I thought of him running through the night, and day until darkness came, before reaching us as we sat by the fire.

"This day is good," the holy man said, "the ancestors did not let you fall down the mountain!"

We both laughed.

"Thank you ancestors!" I yelled, and a bird called back at me.


THE SUN TRAVELED over our heads, went behind the water, and night came down on us. We now walked along a rocky cliff above the waves. Ahead I saw flames from a fire pit, and huts under palm trees. As we got closer, I saw many fishing boats on the sand. The holy man walked beside me, and as the villagers saw us, they walked to join us.

"Welcome!" A man said, and clapped the holy man on his arm.

"It is good to see you!" another man said, and smiled at us.

They walked with us to the fire pit, and sat down. I slipped the heavy basket off, and my back felt good.

"We have much medicine." the holy man told them.

"This is good!" the men said.

Women brought us water, fresh fruit and fish. I was happy to eat, and soon my belly was full.

A man walked to us, the village men let him pass, and he sat down by the holy man.

"I am Kimo."

The holy man smiled, "I have heard of you."

"The chief." I thought, and looked at him.

"You know of my brother?" he asked.

"Yes," the holy man said, "he lives with the ancestors."

"He left the village with many men," Kimo told us, "they wanted to fight, not fish and care for their families."

The village men nodded, some saying "Yes."

Kimo looked around at the villagers, then back at the holy man, "When they returned, they told us of the battle."

The holy man nodded.

"I told them that I am chief now," Kimo said, "and they must fish, and join with women, to make grandchildren for the fathers that lost their sons."

"Good." the holy man said.

"We want peace," Kimo said.

"The other villages also want peace." The holy man told him.

A man gave Kimo strong fruit juice, he handed it to the holy man, and he took a large drink. He smiled, then took another drink, and handed it back to Kimo. Kimo took a large drink, then passed it to the man sitting next to him.

"Kai," the holy man said, and pointed to the huts, "give medicine to the villagers."

I walked from the fire pit, heard the holy man and Kimo, talking and laughing.

"Ancestors, guide me to give medicine." I thought.


I SAW women standing by a hut, and walked to them.

"Do you need medicine?"

They nodded, and I followed them, until we came to a small hut. They took me into a room with flowers, and a bowl of fresh fruits. The hut was well cared for, and an old woman sat on a mat, leaning against the wall. She smiled, and waved me to come.

"Welcome." she said, and put out her arms to me. I leaned down, and her hair smelled fresh from bathing.

"Our mother." A woman told me.

"Sit." the old woman said, and moved her legs so I could sit on the mat.

"Do you need medicine?"

The old woman smiled again, and put her hand on my arm.

"No medicine," she said, "my man is waiting, to take me to the ancestors' village"

"Mother!" a daughter cried out.

I turned to look at the daughter, and she shook her head at me. "She went to her mat, and will not get up."

"She wants a feast!" another daughter said, "so she can leave us."

The daughters were angry, yet, when I looked at the old woman she smiled.

"I will speak with her." I said, and waved them to leave us.

The daughters nodded, and walked out of the hut.

"Grandmother," I said gently, "have you seen their father?"

She smiled, and water came into her eyes, "He is there." and she pointed to the corner of the hut.

"Will you leave soon?" I asked.

She nodded her head.

I closed my eyes, and thought, "What can I do?"

"Give her a feast" my teacher whispered, "with food and family."

I opened my eyes, and smiled. "You will feast, and laugh before you go."

The old woman clapped her hands, "Yes, we will have a feast!"

I stood up, and walked outside and to the daughters.

"Give her a feast," I said, "and have many come."

They looked at me, and I knew they thought I was too young to be a medicine man.

"Give her a feast! She will leave with your father soon." I told them, and saw their mouths open.

I turned and walked away before they could speak. I thought of this old woman, then of my mother. She told us, that her sister waited, to take her away.

"Good" I thought, "we are led by our family to the ancestors' village."

I saw the holy man still speaking with the men at the fire pit, so I

146

walked to more huts, and talked with the women. A young mother called to me, "My son needs medicine."

I walked to her, and she showed me her son, who lay on his back with his head turned to us. His mouth hung open, and his eyes watched us.

"Does he speak?" I asked.

"No," she said, "he does not walk, or feed himself. He is yet a baby."

I put my hand on his forehead, and suddenly saw his mother bringing him in. She bit on a small branch, and pushed hard, yet the child would not come. Women stood next to her, and pushed on her belly. When he finally came from his mother, a rope wrapped around his neck.

I looked at his mother, "Did he breath air after he came from you?"

"No," she said, "my mother took the rope from his neck, then he breathed."

I turned back to him, I had not seen a child such as this, and did not know what medicine would help. I looked into the boy's eyes, and saw how he watched his mother.

"He will pass." My teacher whispered.

"He does not want to leave you," I told his mother, "yet he will pass."

Her eyes filled with water, "my grandmother is with the ancestors, and will care for him."

She rubbed his foot with her hand, and smiled at him. I watched his eyes, they never left her.

"I have no medicine for him." I told her.


I WALKED OUT, and found others that needed medicine for sore bones, and a cut foot. I talked with many people, and was given tea and fruit. I thought how Konani had given talk, and laughter as medicine, so I also did this with each villager that wanted to speak with me. I left the last hut, and walked back to the sand, where the holy man and men still sat by the fire pit.

The holy man turned to me, "A grandmother wants a feast?" he said, and the men laughed.

"She wants a feast before she passes."

He nodded, and looked at me.

"She said her man waits to guide her."

The holy man smiled, then looked at the men, "She will have a feast!"

They laughed, and the chief said, "We will have a feast for you also." and put his hand on the holy man's shoulder.

We ate much fish this night, and the men drank more strong juice. The holy man stood, called to the ancestors to join the fire pit, and many blessings were said for the village. I walked back to the old woman's hut, where many villagers gathered around her. She saw me and waved me in.

"This is a great feast" she said, stretching out her arms to me. I leaned down, and she spoke quietly in my ear.

"Thank you." she smiled at me, I saw that her eyes shined, and she was happy.

She was speaking, and laughing, as I walked out. I turned to look at her from outside the hut, and saw her man waiting behind her.

Water came into my eyes, "She enjoys her feast, and will be glad to leave also."

I stood, watching more, and felt my heart happy for her.

"I will ask for a feast before I pass." I thought, and walked away.

I saw the holy man and Kimo walk to the sand, where they stood speaking. After they returned to the fire pit, the holy man gathered the young men that had been in battle, and spoke to them.

"Are you happy?" he asked them.

"Yes." said a strong young man, with marks on his skin, from the fighting.

"I have a woman and a child." said another.

After following the chief's son to battle, the young warriors were glad to be back.

"We built a new fishing boat," said brothers, "and have caught much fish for the village."

The holy man nodded, "Good."

A young warrior spoke loudly, "The chief's son comes to me."

The holy man looked at him, "Does he speak?"

"He tells me to gather men for battle."

The holy man shook his head, "He must go to the ancestors." the holy man told him.

The young man did not speak.

"Tell him," the holy man yelled, "Go! Do not come back!"

The young man looked at him, and nodded.

"The chief's son cannot lead you to battle again," the holy man said, "Your families need you, and the ancestors protect you,"

"I will say this." the young man told him.

"I am glad you are in the village." the holy man told the young men, "your families are glad also."

I watched their faces, and saw the holy man had blessed these young warriors.


WE SLEPT, then woke to women's voices. The sun was not up, yet light lit the village.

"Our mother has left us!" I heard a woman cry out.

We walked to the old woman's hut, where she lay on her mat. Her eyes were closed, she had passed while she slept.

The holy man spoke to the daughters, "Your mother is with your father."

A daughter kissed her mother's forehead, "I will see you when I pass."

She had peace in her heart, yet the other daughters lay their arms over their mother's body, with water running from their eyes.

"Speak to your mother," the holy man told them, "She is still near and hears you."

He looked at me, "We go."

# CHAPTER 12

We slept again on the narrow trail, and returned to the holy man's camp before dark. I was glad to be back, dropping my basket, to swim in the pool by the river. The holy man swam also, then walked into the trees to speak with the ancestors. I put wood into the fire pit, and fished.

The trees stood quiet and strong, the birds sang, and flew over my head. Fish swam in the river water that moved, without stopping, and shined under the sun. I was with the trees, birds, fish, water and sun. I did not hear sounds of villagers and did not give medicine to them. I heard only my thoughts, and felt only my body. I sat, and looked around the camp. I knew why the ancestors wanted this place. They wanted this peace, they wanted to hear these sounds, and hear the ancestors clearly when they spoke. I thought of when I sat by the waterfall as a boy, when I first listened to my teacher, not knowing then who it was that spoke to me.

THIS NIGHT SITTING at the fire pit, I asked the holy man, "Why do you not give medicine to the villagers?"

He looked at me, "When I was young I gave medicine to the villagers, now I welcome the ancestors to their fire pit."

I thought of this.

"The ancestors guide me to speak to the villagers." he said.

"Do the villagers hear their ancestors?" I asked.

He shook his head, "They will learn when they are ready."

"Will you have another assistant?"

"Yes," he said, and smiled, "we both will."

"I have much to learn!" I told him, knowing I was not ready for an assistant.

"I have much to teach!" he said, and laughed.


WE TALKED of our travels since I joined him.

"You have not stayed in camp like the others," he said, "we have traveled much, and you have seen many villages."

I nodded, "I enjoyed this."

He looked at me, yet did not speak, and I knew he listened to his teacher.

"This will make you ready," he said, "to travel a new path."

"Have you seen this?" I asked.

He smiled, "You will travel much as a medicine man."

I wanted to ask more, yet as I opened my mouth, he stood.

"I will sleep." he said, and walked to his hut.

I watched him leave, then turned back to the fire. The fire was small, with flames now burning low. I wondered where I would travel as a medicine man.

"I will not go to another island," I thought, "he said he would not ask me to leave."

I felt my teacher, and she whispered, "The ancestors guide you."

I did not feel good when I heard this. "I will stay here." I told myself.

Yet inside me, I heard a whisper of the voice that sounded like my own, "You will go."

# ABOUT THE AUTHOR

APRIL AUTRY

April writes about her spiritual journey, including many of her past lives.

April is an Intuitive mentor, Quantum healer, Reiki master, Yoga teacher, and teaches alignment of your mind-body-soul through consciousness expansion and spiritual practices. Books, blog, shop, and services can be found on her website:

https://GalacticGrandmother.com

April enjoys reading your book reviews, so please feel free to email her at:

https://info@galacticgrandmother.com

www.ingramcontent.com/pod-product-compliance
Lightning Source LLC
LaVergne TN
LVHW052027080426
835513LV00018B/2209